3-4

"... and
the criminals
with him ..." Lk 23:33

"…and the criminals with him…" Lk 23:33

a first-person book
about prisons
edited by
Will D. Campbell
and
James Y. Holloway

PAULIST PRESS
New York / Paramus / Toronto

ACKNOWLEDGMENTS

The chapter "Prison" is from RESISTANCE AND CONTEMPLATION by James Douglass. Copyright © 1972 by James W. Douglass. Reprinted by permission of Doubleday & Company, Inc.

The articles in this book were originally published in the 1972 Winter-Spring issue of *Katallagete,* Journal of the Committee of Southern Churchmen, Nashville, Tennessee, © 1972.

Published by Paulist Press
Editorial Office: 1865 Broadway, N.Y., N.Y. 10023
Business Office: 400 Sette Drive, Paramus, N.J. 07652

Printed and bound in the
United States of America

Contents

vi *Contents*

Southern Prison Camps

Marc Hacker

There is currently a great to-do about the evils of prison. But let's face it, prisons are very much needed. Man must have some means of protecting himself from himself. Prisons fulfill this need in that they hide away, they put out of sight, his mistakes with his children. Prisons are monuments to man's lust, avarice, and indifference. Prisons to most onlookers are dark and mysterious places inhabited by persons to be feared. But in many cases they are bright shining jewels of architecture set beautifully into a scenic countryside about which their curious appearing inhabitants move silently, sluggishly and menacingly. Their outward aspects are as varied and as constant as the stars. Man of today, as man of the past, looks upon them in the same way. What he sees is the timelessness of his baser self. He vaguely sees but rarely recognizes a side of himself that is so deeply imbedded within his innate nature as to defy eradication. He sees himself as he might have been in times past. He sees himself as he might be, had he not been denied the training and conditioning necessary to make of him a functional, contributing part of our present definition of social behavior. He sees, but he does not acknowledge.

1

I have above used the word "evils," but I do not like it. I question the existence of evil. I distrust words like "right" and "wrong," "good" and "bad." These are things defined by men in accordance with what *could* be—warped and distorted through fancy, idealism, and ignorance: Concepts of how things *should* be instead of how they *are*. I know only that things are seldom as we think they *should* be, and are more often as they *are*. Convicts generally accept this and make of it the nucleus for a society of their own. Their society is founded on fear of reprisal for having done anything to undermine the fundamental laws that are unwritten, yet more real than any to be found on the lawbooks of society at large. These laws are basically those of hear nothing, see nothing, speak nothing.

Learning to do the things which these laws require, is sometimes a painful knowledge to acquire. A convict then finds making his time to be far easier than he had imagined. And it is here "evil" exists in a prison, if it exists there at all.

I am a white Appalachian, from Manchester, Clay County, Kentucky, reared in that ghetto for economic refugees known as "Little Appalachia" in Cincinnati, Ohio.

I have served several years in confinement and have some knowledge of what prisons are like. I know what it is to be a prisoner of the State. I have served time in two of our western prisons, San Quentin and Folsom, one northern, Indiana (that's northern to me), and two southern. In addition, I have served time in two federal institutions. All have been generally the same. And the counterparts of all the men in each were noted by me to be in each of the others.

Prisons are like western movies: they are, with small, insignificant differences, all the same. When you've experienced one, you've equipped yourself with a foreknowledge of what the next will be. That foreknowledge, however, never seems adequate to allow one to cope with the bestiality, sadism, selfish cruelty, and animalistic attitudes held by those with whom one is caged. These attitudes, as are all aspects within a prison, are more naked and raw in some prisons than in others. This is particularly true in my experience with two prison systems, North Carolina and Virginia. Both systems are similar in that they are comprised of one small, central prison which serves as a maximum security lockup and a clearing station for assignment of convicts to one of the many road camps scattered strategically throughout the state. These camps are small, inconspicuous units hidden away in some sparsely populated area. They are basically comprised of a cell block, a clothes house, a wash house, a "hole" and a mess hall. All of which is surrounded and enclosed by one or more tall wire fences topped with barbed wire. These camps are governed individually by a Corrections Officer with a rank of Lieutenant or Captain. And their attitude toward treatment of felons and their charge is usually one of despotism. They were, and in the main still are, men adhering to the old chaingang ideology. Their belief is that they are God in their camps and screw those idiots at CP. CP is a term denoting Central Prison from which they receive the orders, at which they sneer and scoff.

For example, the first camp to receive my attention was the one located at and in the small town of Clinton, North Carolina. It was at that time (1961) governed by a diminutive old man tortured by advanced arthritis, known to the men on his camp only as "Captain Hooks." The aptness of his name amused me later, but on that day of my first making his acquaintance, I was not amused. Neither was he. He, as was usually the case, took quick notice of my arrogance and lack of humility. So his words to me prior to my going behind the fence were hard, sure and certain. "Hacker," he said, "I don't give one goddamn who or what you are and I don't give a fuck whether or not you live or die. All I give a damn about is my camp. After today, you will probably not see me again. At least you'd better hope you don't. I never go inside that fence unless I have to. And if I have to, somebody loses some of their ass. Like I say, I just care about my camp. When you get inside, you can do like you want—you can smoke, gamble, screw or be screwed, suck or be sucked— just don't saw on my bars. And meet me at the gate ready for a day's work every morning."

His was a memorably shocking and accurate speech. He meant every word of it. We could do, and many did, the things that he said I would be "free" to do. We met him at the gate most assiduously, also.

I stayed at Clinton approximately a year. The living conditions were abominable, the food almost intolerable and the work back-breaking labor with picks, shovels, axes and bush-axes. The gang foreman and shotgun guards were merciless in heat and cold. Yet, there was virtually no grumbling and complaining. The mood of the men was always light and cheerful. That old bastard "Hooks" knew how to conquer the simple souls in his charge and he made the best of that knowledge. Although I myself understood it, I was always in a state of wonder about the ability of men to *endure* (that was the word for me, but not for them: the caged and watched-over life of a chain-gang-without-the-chains convict) so light-heartedly and ever joyously.

I transferred from Clinton to another camp located near another small town called Hillsboro, North Carolina. In order to prevent its convicts from becoming bored, or as they, the convicts, put it, "burned-out" with life, officials will generally, upon request by a convict in writing, transfer him to a camp of his choice. I had definitely become "burned-out" with Clinton and was more than ready to make a change. I chose to request a transfer to Hillsboro on the basis of the personal recommendations of some acquaintances at Clinton. It was thus that I discovered that I would most like a camp they considered a "bad" one instead one they considered a "good" one. They evaluated a camp by the degree of its looseness in the cell block. Therefore, a camp that was more disciplined and permitted less gambling, drinking and homosexuality was a *bad* one. One that permitted more of these things was a *good* one. Well, although I considered myself a con-wise son-of-a-bitch, they put one over on me in my ignorance of their standards of these things.

So one bright day in the fall of '62, the Blue Goose pulled up out front and I was loaded aboard completely decked out in my leg chains, step chains and restraining belt around my waist with my hands handcuffed to it. Blue Goose is a bus owned and operated by the North Carolina prison system for the sole purpose of picking up and depositing convicts from one point in the state to another. This sometimes involves transporting a man several hundred miles over by-roads between points no further distant from one

another along a direct route than fifty or sixty miles.
It frequently means a stop overnight at CP and the
taking of another bus to complete the trip. This was
the case with me. It's but about fifty miles between
Clinton and Raleigh, North Carolina, but I had a
bruised and sore ass from riding that hard-seated bus
all that day through and about the countryside before
reaching Raleigh, where I had to lay over that night
before going on to Hillsboro the next day.

Then at Raleigh, there is a section of cells set
aside for men enroute between camps. This section
is called the Shipping Quarter. It is one of the major
communications points between prisoners. It is the
clearinghouse for messages put on the grapevine. It
is the place where violators of convict law are frequently punished and it is where punishments, ordered for commuting convicts, are sent out in every
direction. A punishment that is certain eventually
to reach its target.

At the time of my transfer from Clinton to Hillsboro, I instinctively looked over my companions.
They are often dangerous. As my eyes and senses
examined them one by one I took particular notice
of one little fellow looking as if he would give an
arm or leg to be elsewhere. I passed him by to finish
my inspection and came back to him to watch and
wonder as he furtively cast his eyes about unseeingly.
He was obviously keenly aware of a danger. I could
detect no one threatening him by look or actions so
I surmised his fear to be based on some knowledge
becoming known to us that he wanted very much to
keep a secret. I was concerned about him. I hoped he
would be put into a cell with me on Shipping Quarter. But his fate, or the grapevine, finally caught him
that night and there was nothing I could do to help.

Shameful as it may seem, I was adhering to the un-written laws—see nothing, hear nothing, speak no-thing. Perhaps he would have been more lucky had he not been so articulate: I say that because I could hear the muted voices as he talked with his cell mate. At least the punishment meted out so brutally to him that night would have been delayed and he could have conceivably escaped it altogether. As it was, he was beaten mercilessly until his blood flowed glisteningly in the dim prison light from out of his cell onto the tier outside. I could see the blood and hear his low moans of pain and agony following each thudding blow that fell upon his small body. It went on for long moments. The moans ceased, but the blows continued to thud, interminably it seemed. Then it all grew quiet and finally a guard appeared. He left, and soon several more arrived accompanied by two convicts from the dispensary with a stretcher.

Later, lying in my bunk, I thought about the seeming indifference and cruelty of it. I could see so many ways of preventing such things and I cursed into hell all the bastards who could do something about it, and wouldn't. I cursed them all from the governor right on down to the turnkey.

The next morning I was put aboard another Goose and taken on to Hillsboro. It is, physically, a replica of Clinton. There was no "Captain Hooks," however. In fact, there was no Captain by any name to meet us as we alighted from the bus. We were hustled gruffly into the compound, and upon looking around, I saw the place to be physically the same as Clinton. It had the same number of buildings, and they were of like construction to those at Clinton. The only difference I could see at that time was one of location and setting. It sat atop a gently sloping hill or huge knoll and was shaded in summer by large oaks and chestnut trees. In summer it gave one the feeling experienced when reading the lushness of *Falcon Hurst.* In winter, the barren bleakness reminds one of *The Return of the Native.*

My arrival there coincided with the advent of the barren bleakness and it was an unhappy time for me. Added to this were the conditions inside that cell block. It was identical to Clinton in excesses in drinking, gambling, and homosexuality. But here, too, were things not to be found in Clinton. Here there were narcotics and dope and the consequential warped emotions that resulted in knifings, forcible rapes, fights with clubs and fists. Young men were forcibly made to submit to gang orgies of sodomy and oral sexual gratification, and then reviled, beaten and made to "check out,"—a procedure that meant they must upon threats of pain, serious injury or death, give the Captain the option of transferring them or putting them into the "hole" without giving him a reason. No reason, *just get me out!* The Captain knew, though: the guards knew and he knew. The guards would make their rounds outside the cell blocks, look in the windows, and see the things of which I speak, laugh, make obscene gestures and walk away to joke about it later with other guards and convicts.

In some way, not clearly understood by me, I have always had what must be a remarkable respect and regard from convicts. As I have indicated, I am arrogant and have no humility. I could not and did not hesitate to let my feelings be known. Yet they, the convicts, respected me and did not get in my way. They were curiously considerate of me and at times this was laughable. For example, the bunks

were double-deckers placed in lots of four; that is,
two double-deckers placed side by side and a divid-
ing space of about twelve inches, then another set
of four bunks as described, and so on. The bottom
two of these sets of bunks were usually occupied by
a boy and his daddy. The upper bunks would be
occupied by men who did not play the game. I had
an upper bunk. A man couldn't get much rest there
because the boy and his daddy would keep the bunk
in an animated and an agitated state until the wee
hours. The bunks were, by reason of age, long use
and other factors, very rickety. The boy and his
daddy's homosexual activities, the necessary movement and coupling made things rough for those of
us on the top bunks. Anyway, many a boy has gotten out of his bunk to look sheepishly at me, and
many a daddy has come to me to apologize, beg my
pardon, excuse himself with a "you-know-how-it-is"
—as if I really *did* know how it was, despite my telling him and others that I thought them to be some
kind of slimy bastards that must have crawled from
under some rock. I sometimes felt that they thought
my criticisms to be complimentary. They've laughed
heartily at me and told me a man is not a man until
he's known the pleasures of a boy's ass. I'd laugh
with them and deride them jestingly in the light of
day, for I knew the things they did were not uncommon, anywhere. The only real difference in their
indulgences as compared with the same kind practiced
by men on the outside is that those outside are more
covered and discrete, whereas those in prison had of
necessity to be more overt.

Hillsboro finally got to me. I saw myself nearing
a point of irritability because of conditions there,
my failure to make a parole when I felt I deserved

one, and an intuitive feeling that I was close to
losing a love of the only girl that I had ever really
loved. I feared I might well lose my temper and kill
someone or be killed. To avert this state of emotions
within myself, I began to consider escape. This led
to myself and two others evolving a plan to make a
key for the squad truck, the truck we rode to and
from the camp on workdays. All of us were under
the gun. That is, all of us worked together on a gang
or squad that was guarded with one or more twelve-
gauge shotguns, short guns or side arms. Our plan
was simple, and it required some nerve, a lot of
patience in the trial and error method of making
a key for the truck, endurance and stamina if we
succeeded in the initial steps, and a lot of luck in
the immediate hours following the taking of the truck.

It took us approximately a month to perfect a key
made from a pocket knife blade. The way we made
it was to file a bit on it night after night, take it on
the road with us the next day, and while "making
water" alongside the truck, insert the key in the
ignition to see if it would turn. I happened to be the
one "pouring it out" and testing the key when the
thing turned smoothly and the lovely red lights denoting oil pressure and temperature lighted up on
the truck dash. I quickly notified my fellow con-
spirators that we were in the money and suggested
there was no better time than then to move. They
agreed.

I didn't want to drive, I had been away from cars
and trucks too long. I elected one of the others to
drive. It had just begun to drizzle and that made
things ideal. It made the guards and foreman uncomfortable and in that month of late October, it
made their minds wander to warm food and beds.

It made the air damp and this made it difficult for a dog to follow our scent. Now, if we could just get that truck under way without getting our heads blown off. . . .

The rain began to fall a bit harder and we were ordered to put away our tools and load up. The squad moved from the road bank where we had been cutting right-of-way toward the truck. We had a guard with a shotgun flanking us on the right and the foreman with a short gun flanking us on the left. At the truck, the guard was behind us and the foreman in front. We gave our tools to another man to put away for us. We then hollered "pouring it out!" and the guard motioned for us to go ahead. We then approached the front of the truck along both sides. I opened the door on the right, and the other two opened the door on the driver's side. They stood side by side, one slightly nearer the truck than the other. The one nearest the ignition inserted the key and switched it on as we pretended to pass water.

When the red lights flashed on, I gave the signal and all three of us leaped into the truck seat. Billy quickly started the engine. I sat transfixed. The engine stalled, the foreman who could see us plainly half raised his gun, let it fall, and began running toward us. Billy again started the engine, he let out the clutch and we began to move. As we slowly, agonizingly, gained speed, the foreman made a leap for the side door on the driver's side. He missed and we were on the way.

Our escape was successful. I found a job and went to work. Billy and the other fellow didn't. I remained at large for a bit over two and one-half years. Billy and the other fellow . . . I don't know.

On March 5, 1966, while still a fugitive, I fell

approximately sixty feet from a steel beam to the ground below. I was working on a construction project. The fall very nearly killed me. I suffered five breaks in my back, six in my pelvic area, a broken left hip and a broken left leg. I had been in the hospital ten weeks when on Friday, May 13, 1966, I was visited by a neatly dressed man carrying a briefcase. He had found his way to me by reason of a man having robbed a bank in Rock Hill, South Carolina, of $43,000 and escaping. It was thought he escaped in a red car. I owned a red car which had attracted the attention of the FBI as they passed by and saw it. They knew, of course, that I could not have participated in the robbery. However, they did think I might know whether or not the car had been used in the robbery and by whom.

At any rate, that interview was the end of my freedom. They ran a make on me using only my description and it came back with my life history. They immediately returned me to prison in Raleigh.

In the above related experiences, I have given whoever reads them a shallow but accurate idea of what it is like to be a convict in Southern and all prisons. Reading it can, and I hope will, be something like looking beyond the surface of a stream into the depths below. I hope you can see in what I have written some of the rocks—their blunt, abrasive, and sharp edges, which abound in the stream of prison life.

It is a curious and unusual stream. Its spring and fall is wherever there is a prison the world over. It possesses a degree of sameness that is to me frightening. It somehow personifies that eternal sameness of man himself. It has a quickness about it, too, which is somehow mindful of the quickness of life.

If one, getting caught in its ebb and flow, is not terribly alert, it will swallow one as inexorably and completely as, in the end, do one's years.

Security and Rehabilitation and God in a Godless World

A. Puchalski

Few people are familiar with the psychological structure of a maximum security prison with its disciplined thoroughness. Fewer still can begin to comprehend the effects of certain aspects of contemporary prison life or that it might actually be more harsh and brutal than that practiced in our early American prison system with its physical punishment. And only those closely associated with our prison system are aware of the absoluteness of power wielded by prison officials to exact obedience from the wards entrusted to their care by the courts. It is a system that represents absolute totalitarianism, with no power or control in the hands of any convict faction, but rather in the hands of our keepers.

The most painful condition imposed upon a man in prison is the loss of liberty. Life becomes frustrating in the extreme. Not only do the walls serve as a grim, constant reminder of the restrictions and isolation that a man is subjected to, they literally serve as a barrier that separates the world of the living—from that of the dead. The numberless hours that hang like overripe fruit on a tree, by-passed by the harvester to decay and waste, magnify the loss and frustration.

Your great, big, wonderful world suddenly shrinks to a mere few acres of space where every movement and action is controlled by the puppeteer who seldom loosens the rein to permit too much freedom of movement. The months pass by agonizingly slow and the nagging fact that your confinement represents a deliberate rejection by society stings deeply. The isolation is complete, for the frightening realization soon dawns upon you that not only did society confine you to a prison—but within it as well.

With the stabbing pain of each deprivation imposed a man ofttimes wonders just where he is going to find strength to persevere. Some don't. The bareness of the cell in which you're confined: your *home,* the absence of even a single piece of furniture that you might call your own, the traditional striped trousers and uniformity of dress—the overwhelming loss of identity, is stifling. Such is prison life.

Prisons have been built with only one thought in mind: Security. The comfort and welfare of the inmate who would be required to inhabit the dungeons were for the most part ignored. This is evidenced by the Bastille-like structure erected in the 1790's at my prison, that provides a cell measuring five by nine feet, or forty-five square feet of space per man. Here, we are required to spend on the average sixteen hours of every day—for the most part, vegetating.

But there is a far greater ugliness than that which meets the eye of the observer in the greyness of the walls that separate the two worlds. It is an invisible ugliness with more far-reaching consequences than those achieved in the medieval Star Chambers—brutalization; dehumanization of men; an ugly system implemented for the sole purpose of manifesting that absoluteness of power to force men to their knees in submission—in the interest of security.

It is painfully stressed by the administration of our prisons that decision-making is no longer a function of a convict and that his most basic needs can only be attended to . . . by the grace of his benevolent keepers. This, then, is the beginning of our psychological annihilation; the suppression of independent thought; the reliance on our keepers to resolve all decisions for us. Serf-like dependency.

Dehumanization begins with the complete indifference of the keepers towards their charges. In addition to the strict administrative policy forbidding "fraternizing" with inmates, far too many prison guards treat their positions as nothing more than jobs and refuse to extend themselves to help an inmate in trouble. Their attitudes are basically one of contempt and that of master to slave, disregarding even our basic human rights. This attitude changes somewhat to a paternalistic one when dealing with informers.

While lack of any meaningful communication between keeper and kept is the greatest obstacle preventing understanding and therefore negating any program instituted to assist in the inmate's rehabilitation, it is but one of a series of policies deliberately imposed to accomplish a servile attitude in the inmates.

Fear produces submission; thus, if we brutalize a man, strip him of self-worth, denigrate him not only in his own eyes, but the eyes of his peers, we create an automaton: a *model convict*. But also of importance, only then can a rigid, uniform society be moulded for easier control.

To accomplish this goal every inmate upon arrival at our prison has his head shaved bald. He is dressed in a denim, sack-cloth uniform without regard for fitting and cast into a cell, the size of which I mentioned earlier; furnished with a cot, cast-iron toilet and a solitary chair. He is also issued one bar of soap, a roll of tissue paper and a scrub brush. He is reminded in no uncertain terms that the soap and tissue must last him a full month between issues—at which time he can receive more *if* he asks the officer for another issue. Dependence is emphasized.

During this quarantine or *conditioning* period that usually lasts two weeks, the inmate will seldom leave his cell, exercise, mingle socially with other convicts or participate in the inmate functions. His entire world centers around that nine-by-five cubicle and the occasional click of the guard's key in the lock which will give him a few minutes of freedom that comes when he is called out for interviews and physical exams. After spending an average of twenty-two hours a day in his cell, it isn't difficult to understand why the man starts becoming withdrawn in his manner. The system leaves very little room for resistance.

Few social contacts with the world beyond the prison walls are fostered, even to the extent that we are permitted to write only ten letters a month. Outside groups are frowned upon when they visit the prison—such contact only serves to remind those in the world of the condemned of freedom and loved ones, and to the visitor, the conditions of our environment. It serves to undermine the dehumanizing process and cannot be tolerated.

With the passing of time it is inevitable that most men succumb to the system and integrate themselves into the sub-culture of prison life. In doing so, civilized behavior and moral responsibility are shed and replaced with prison standards considered socially acceptable. Love and kindness are looked upon as weaknesses and *might* becomes *right*. Sexual perversion is an acceptable behavior, and the tough guy is admired with envy. It is a society where the weak are sacrificed to the strong to maintain the status quo, always with the approval of the prison administrators who know that by placating the tough guy and trouble-maker their own jobs become easier.

Despite, or perhaps I should say in spite of, the all-out campaign by prison officials to suppress autonomy in our inmate society and to control every movement, a sub-culture does exist. It is a culture that excludes all but convicts and is as orderly in structure as any free-world community. It lacks a duly elected governing body to represent it, but this is only because of the prison officials' stubborn refusal to recognize any degree of independence. Nevertheless, there is a *de facto* recognition by the inmate population of certain *leaders* amongst them, men who are usually considered anti-administration by both the prison officials and inmates. Resistance to authority is sufficient to qualify a man for candidacy.

In the midst of what would to a layman's eyes be interpreted as a confused mass, there is organization. True, just as the prison officials' every effort is directed at dehumanization, the convicts' is structured to oppose, undermine and compromise—thus, in that respect the convict culture is one that is dia-

metrically opposed to the principles free society
lives by. It is easy then to understand that a man
spending a considerable period of time in such an
environment suffers irreparable psychological damage
and is hardly qualified to re-enter the society that
once declared him an outcast.

Little time and effort are expended in teaching
the inmate a vocational trade. The sad fact is that no
vocational program exists at most prisons in America to which a man could apply himself. In terms of
education, until recently when some college programs
commenced, acquiring a primary education was a
dubious endeavor. What alternatives are left for
those who come to prison alone and whose families
have deserted them or are unable to send them a
few dollars every month?

As in any free community, ours too, offers di-
verse vocations to be pursued: gambling, narcotic
peddling, shylocking (money-lending), homosexuality and strong-arming, just to mention a few. And it
shouldn't sound strange that the men pursue these
vocations with as much determination as their free-
world counterparts. They have no other method of
providing for the basic necessities like toothpaste,
soap and tobacco. While it is true that approximately
half the population at my prison, or six hundred
men, are assigned to work in the State Shops and
earn fifty cents a day, the average inmate makes, at
best, fourteen dollars a month. This is hardly sufficient to provide for the things he needs. Consequently,
he chooses one of the above-mentioned *professions*
and pushes any thought of rehabilitation to the back
of his mind. Where his initial misadventure with the
law might have been an unfortunate incident, it
now becomes one of *choice*.

Sexual perversion requires some specific understanding because of the prevalent misunderstanding
of it by those outside prison. Until most recently, the
public's view of prison life had been a distorted one,
with little sympathy for the needs of the incarcerated felon—be they material or sexual in nature.
With the growing failure of our penal systems, however, society has been responding with interest by
studying existing conditions in our institutions.

Homosexuality is present on every level of
America's penal systems. It is just not possible to
incarcerate men for any length of time and subject
them to a state of celibacy. Sooner or later, the pressures of imprisonment will force most of them to
seek sexual gratification in whatever manner is available. In terms of right and wrong, it is as inhuman
to subject men to forced abstinence as it is for these
same men to indulge in what society still considers
a reprehensible act.

The evil of the sexual perversions which mani-
fest themselves in our men in prison does not lie with
their indulgence, but rather that of subjecting the
younger prisoners into forced homosexuality. For it
is those in the age group nineteen to twenty-five, the
young and ignorant convict, who is most susceptible
to be chosen as a homosexual partner. Others, deserted by friends and family, sell themselves into
homosexuality to ward off hunger, and to provide
for the basic necessities of prison life.

Homosexual rapes aren't nearly as uncommon as
the public is given to believe. Sex-starved men, many
of whom were originally convicted of sex crimes and
required to endure many years in prison, have little
concern for a youngster serving two or three years.
And the youth will not retaliate for fear of having

his sentence enlarged. Thus the courts commit these men to prison as petty burglars and drug addicts—and our prisons return them to society as sex deviates.

It would appear at first glance that the convict's subversion of the ugly dehumanizing system is successful and therefore, few men become ensnared in its web. To the contrary, for while in some respects that might hold true, the sub-culture, permeated with anti-social attitudes is far from conducive to rehabilitation. At best, it serves the interests of the long-term incorrigible who has long ago lost all hope of release, while at the same time it destroys all positive attitudes in the younger convict, the first offender who could ordinarily still be salvaged. It is here that society is failing most miserably.

A serious question arises at this juncture. How is it possible at all to undermine a system that is totalitarian in nature? Since the majority of most prison populations is only average in intelligence and the keeper's power complete, we can only assume that the sub-culture is permitted and perhaps needed by prison officials to maintain order and discipline. It is certain that security has top priority over all other functions in prison; and to maintain a tight security system without pushing the convict populace into open rebellion, diversions are necessary—or more apropos, *perversions are necessary for security.*

When viewed in retrospect, little hope can be held out for our penal system and the methods employed to deal with criminal offenders. An entirely new concept must be implemented, one with less emphasis on brain-washing a man into submission. Rehabilitation that must depend on the lash is soon discarded the moment the man takes his first step through the prison doors and into the free world.

There is a solution which, if properly executed, can have a marked effect on the present day crime problem. Success or failure will depend on the co-operation of those handling "custody," and the sociologists who at present have made little headway in explaining away the crime epidemic that is sweeping our country.

The first and major step is to destroy the "no fraternizing" policy so stringently enforced in our penal system today. Unless keeper and kept can establish a common bond through which they might relate to one another, the authority of the badge will continue to draw resentment. Group therapy sessions (voluntary, of course) where both sides are permitted to speak out freely not only opens the door to understanding, but permits the inmate to vent frustrations otherwise considered offensive and that could net him a disciplinary report.

It is equally important to remove restrictive policy that prevents outside groups from entering the prison and mingling with the inmate body. To this extent "custody" must be prepared to revamp its policies and thoughts. Security-minded officials who refuse to modify their thinking to conform with the new school of thought must be replaced with more open-minded men.

There is absolutely no sense in isolating men, ninety percent of whom will be returning to the communities they left. Nor is it wise in denying them some social contact that will keep them abreast of current events during their period of incarceration. At present we are nothing but social misfits who find it impossible to fit ourselves into what have now become strange surroundings. Something might also be done about the conditions which encourage homosexuality. Pressure could be brought on legislators to enact laws that will segregate those in the age-group of nineteen to twenty-five from the long-term, hard-core element we find in every prison. But society would be done a far greater service, and at the same time virtually wipe out homosexuality in our prisons, if conjugal visits were permitted.

Can such programs be commenced in prisons considered the country's eyesores; in prisons built over one hundred and fifty years ago to accommodate six hundred men and which presently house twelve hundred? Hardly, unless the archaic living conditions are brought up to date, and not until the present apathetic administration with its old school of "thought methodists" are replaced with something more conducive to rehabilitation. Until then, American prisons will continue to serve as nothing more than a convict factory—turning out *educated* criminals.

Now for some thoughts on a dimension of prison life seldom discussed or written about: few people concern themselves with a convict's spiritual needs. To most, he is an outcast to be hidden away in dungeons, called prisons, supposedly to repent of his sins. There he is stripped of his name and given a number, subjected to the vilest indignities devised by man, and quite often, long after he has paid his debt to society, he must still carry his moral cross of crucifixion with the stigma of being called an *ex-con.*

The attitude is an old, familiar one and is understandable where a gullible and apathetic public is concerned—until the finger of accusation begins to single out the clergy: "the shepherds of the flock."

At such times I can't help but recall from my

childhood memory, a verse of Scripture from the Book of Matthew: "I was in prison, and ye came unto me." Suddenly my mind races over twenty years of my adult life which have been spent behind various prison walls, and I discover that I can count those visits on the fingers of one hand! It almost sounds absurd that a society would confine a man to many years in prison for the purpose of teaching him to repent of his waywardness—and simultaneously neglect to provide the necessary facilities and programs to attain that goal.

When one contemplates the role of the clergy and their failure in responding to the needs of the incarcerated felon, it isn't difficult to come away impressed that they are forbidden from entering our prisons and making contact with its inhabitants. Of course that is not so, but then, where are those whom Jesus commanded: "Go ye therefore and teach . . ."? To whom did he preach these words? For whose benefit?

Are a young drug addict of nineteen, a burglar of twenty-two, a murderer of fifty, too old for redemption? Or are we like *lepers,* too *unclean* to be approached? Perhaps we should raise our eyes to Calvary and look at His two companions in death for the answer.

Many men arriving at prison are hurt not only physically but spiritually, although most would conceal their spiritual hurt. To do otherwise would only subject them to the scorn and ridicule of their fellow inmates. Others spend lonely weeks and months in county jails hoping beyond hope for a visit from their pastors and other community church groups of which many had been members prior to their incar-

lift their spirits when the world is crumbling around them. But no one comes, or is concerned enough to suffer the uncomfortable feeling of approaching —much less entering—a prison. How uncomfortable then must it be for those who languish within its confines.

Forsaken by family and friends, rejected by the society they so wronged, we wander like lost sheep until finally, for lack of adequate religious guidance we become mired in lust and perversion that so abounds in prisons—originally the principal cause of our incarceration. This is a sad reflection indeed on those entrusted to preach from the pulpits the lesson of brotherly love. Is it any wonder why so many men reject the outstretched hand and look upon it with suspicion when finally it is extended?

This is not to say that men in prison are without some religious representation. To the contrary, Catholic and Protestant services are scheduled for every Sunday, Bible classes and religious tracts are available in abundance; religious medals and rosaries are yours for the asking. Salvation of the *Spirit* is the theme—but little, if anything is said of our *Physical* needs.

The call for religious revival reverberates every Sunday from pulpits, to fall on deafened ears of men who cannot identify with impersonal voices gushing what has now become meaningless rhetoric. Regrettable is the fact that most preachers are completely unaware that the greatest wealth of revival material are the inmates—if only they would descend from their ivory towers and approach them on a man-to-man basis. Religion in prison has become a cold and emotionless ritual that should leave no ceration. They seek a familiar face, a kind word to

doubt in anyone's mind as to the reason for low attendance.

Of what practical value is a Bible to me (except to roll cigarettes when I run out of paper?) when I need someone from my home town to keep me informed about my ailing children? Or how can the Sermon on the Mount help a youngster who is on the verge of committing suicide and cannot find someone to trust and who might be in a position to help him? But who is first on the scene to administer the last rites at death?

It seems almost unnatural that our clergymen, evangelists and Christian teachers should segregate themselves from their flocks. It is here, in prison, that most men are vulnerable to religious indoctrination. It would be very foolish to believe that a twenty year-old youth could be so callous as not to have remorse for the crime he committed. Or that even the *hard core* convict has no use for kind words. It was this type of attitude initially that created the existing communication gap and unless something is done to bridge it, many men, particularly the younger set, will continue falling by the wayside.

Most members of the clergy seem to feel that quoting Scripture from memory and spouting off a lot of silly numbers ends their obligation to their fellow man. Seldom do I hear anyone refer to spiritual guidance as an integral part of a man's rehabilitation. Little, if any emphasis is placed on religious guidance for men being released from prison. And few Christians are willing to come forward to embrace an ex-convict in true Christian fellowship—without the "Jesus Saves" overtone. How often are *ex-cons* invited to participate in church socials?

During my many years of incarceration I have

spent what would amount to at least four years in
solitary confinement. At such times my only com-
panion was a Bible which I have read and re-read.
How great were the emotional conflicts that arose to
challenge my distorted social and spiritual values!
Many were the tears I shed in frustration and shame
in those solitary cells where I groveled in confusion
and youthful ignorance, to emerge time and again
full of cynicism. I must admit that the Bible served
its purpose—it occupied my time even if it didn't do
a damned thing for spirit or empty stomach. I wasn't
converted, I didn't see the *light,* and it has only
served to further shake my belief in God. One can
hardly expect our youth to practice love and kindness
in an environment that is shunned by those who
preach it.

Convicts are not heathens and atheists who denounce any need or the existence of a Supreme Being.
We are people, human beings—your husbands, sons
and brothers; alienated perhaps from our Maker, and
now as it would appear, from our fellow man; adrift
in a wilderness of confusion. We are not the carica-
tures portrayed on Hollywood movie screen—mental
defectives incapable of loving, to be treated like wild
beasts without souls. We are mere victims of our
foolish follies, separated from our free brethren by
no more than the grace of God, "for all have
sinned. . . ."

Few people are aware of the harsh and oppres-
sive conditions of prison life and adopt the negative
attitude of letting someone else worry about our
needs—our social leprosy is too ugly for them to
bear. But if our incarceration is to be at all meaningful to us as a lesson in deterrence, it must consist
of more than the lash, cruelty and cold indifference.

There must be a contact established with our communities, especially the religious groups, to allay our many fears of the unknown that will surely confront us upon our return to society. After many years of living strict, regimented lives in an environment where decision-making is almost non-existent, transacting a small purchase, even ordering from a menu in a restaurant, can create uncertainty and prove complex to many men.

There must also be material as well as spiritual support, since both are interrelated. Responsible community businessmen must be ready—nay, eager, to extend their Christian fellowship to us with offers of employment. But of greater importance they must be ready to enter our prisons, to observe first hand the conditions we live under, to familiarize themselves with their less fortunate brethren and to study their needs. In essence, to disseminate that Christian fellowship.

To establish such a relationship, to close the communication gap that is growing ever wider, the clergy is responsible for laying the foundation and must accept the burden of taking us into their folds and forget the traditional excuse that we are not in their parish. Is it not written that "For where two or three are gathered. . . ."? Is a lost lamb no longer part of the flock from which it has strayed, and will not the shepherd leave the hundred and search for the one? Or are these mere flowery words, to be read on Sundays and quickly forgotten?

It is difficult to welcome the prodigal son home with open arms. Too frequently people forget that no man is perfect and to err is human, even unto seventy times seven. And yet, it is the errant, not the righteous, who need guidance. Christianity acknowledges human failure; can man do less than accept this precept in dealing with his brother? Would he deny to those most in need of redemption the right to stand in the shadow of the Cross? How long will our brothers, so blessed with plenty, require us to suffer the cold, begging for spiritual alms?

Society must stop viewing the convict as some denizen, and prison as a place where lawbreakers are housed until their time is up. Punishment without rehabilitation is futile and serves no constructive purpose. And rehabilitation is more than a Sunday church service with a preacher extolling his charges to virtue while he waves a fire brand of hell and damnation for evildoers—then disappears until the following Sunday.

Religion is an integral part of that rehabilitation process which begins not when a man is released, but the day he is delivered to the prison. It is then that he is most apt to respond to practical spiritual overtures, founded not so much on Scripture-quoting, but on Christian fellowship, if he is to comprehend the error of his ways. Only this way will he feel secure in the knowledge that while society is ready to punish evildoers, it is equally prepared to forgive and not harbor resentments.

Are our "souls" the only concern of the clergy? Are they not also an integral part of our personality, our "human-beingness"? Is the quality of a convict's soul less worthy and deserving of salvation than that of another Christian? Are not our physical needs to maintain health in body and mind equally as great?

I urge you to keep your Bibles, tracts, medals and organ music. Instead, give us of yourselves, your time and help just as He gave of Himself to the sick and poor and needy. Come out from behind your cloaks of hypocritical self-righteousness and wallow a while with us thieves, pimps, drug addicts and murderers.

If religious training is in fact an integral part of rehabilitation and our Christian brothers continue keeping themselves aloof from the men in prison, then let me be the first to proclaim that GOD IS DEAD!

Doin' Time

Jane Kennedy

Prisoners learn a great deal in the course of "doin' time." The Department of Corrections calls it "correction," the Treatment Department in prisons seems to believe it is "rehabilitation," but the prisoner knows it as the vengeance of a cruel and insensate society.

In prison one learns to lie to personnel who want to hear what makes them look good. One learns to show child-like obeisance to nervous personnel who know only the ultimate punishment—isolation of the prisoner. One comes to believe the frequently cited maxim, "If this turns out well, it's to my credit; if it doesn't, it's the prisoners' fault."

Dental Laboratory

The Dental Laboratory is a case in point. The man in charge of the teaching wanted the dental technicians to make technical aids to denture-fitting in a certain way. However, the dentist, for whom the aids were constructed, wanted them completed in a different way. When we repeatedly explained this to our teacher, he would become enraged and insist

31

we do it *his* way. Time and again he would tell us that there was only *one* right way, *his* way. The dentist who received the work would become angry with the technicians because, once again, they hadn't produced what he asked them to.

Sometimes the teacher would rearrange teeth in a wax set-up after the technicians had completed the work; he would insist they be taken to the dentist as he had arranged them. The dentist would call this shoddy work and blame the prisoner. Once when he refused to use the work, the teacher became angry with the prisoners for "rearranging" his work.

The teacher also insisted we follow his procedure for denture processing—which procedure invariably led to poorly fitting dentures. Before he came to the staff, the prisoners had learned a step called "burning down the baseplate," which assured proper fit. But the teacher forbade them to use it because it didn't work! If the prisoners didn't do it his way, they had to live with their fellow inmates' poorly fitting dentures. And they were pained as the prisoner paid $25.00 for loose teeth.

The dissension was so great that a series of meetings was held last August. Among them, the technicians met with the Superintendent, who heard their complaints, but insisted that he would always find for the authority figure against the prisoner. In time, administrative policies were changed to decrease friction among the professional personnel. But nothing changed for the prison technicians.

So the burden for being cushions for the professionals grew heavier and heavier. Finally, the prisoners had to take some action and asked for a meeting with the supervising nurse. Their complaints were clearly stated and the removal of the teacher was requested. A progress report was requested in a week. The nurse responded that they had told her all this before. The teacher became very upset when the prisoners talked back to him. The prisoners responded that he had told them many times that he was an old man and just wanted to be obeyed; nevertheless, they insisted that there were things he asked them to do that were simply wrong and he had to be so informed.

The nurse said she wouldn't mind if they wanted to write any other persons about the situation. So they sent the following letter to the Superintendent: "It is imperative that we see you as soon as possible. We think you should be made aware of the impending future of your Dental Laboratory." The four technicians' names were written on it.

The following day, one of the technicians was called to the Director of the Women's Division and was asked by her who wrote the note addressed to the Superintendent. The technician refused to tell her and explained that only the writer might be blamed if she were known. It was an effort of all the technicians who were going to act, and they wanted to be treated as a group. The Director said that she didn't like group participation, and "no one else here does either." She complained that the technicians were trying to pull the teacher down with their nonprofessional opinions. She then told the technician, "you should handle all of this as an individual problem."

The technician replied, "It's not an individual problem, it's a group problem."

The Director replied, "Well, you'd look better handling it in an individual manner."

The technician, now grim, said, "We're going to

stick together." The Director said, "Well, that's what you say!"

The next day, a senior matron appeared in the Dental Laboratory and told the technicians that they were to accompany her to the punishment cottage. Three of the technicians went immediately. A fourth asked if they were to be put in "reflection" (isolation and one meal a day, no visitors, no letters even to lawyers), and the matron said that she didn't know. So the fourth technician refused to walk to an undeserved punishment and five policemen (male guards) were called to take her there. Each of the first three technicians appeared before the discipline board, who asked them about the note written to the Superintendent, put them in Triple O overnight and they were given other jobs the next day.

The fourth technician was put in "the hole" for five days. When she was freed, she asked the Deputy Superintendent why she was put in the hole. She was told that is was because she had refused to obey an order (walking to punishment). She also was given another job a week later.

Intimidations

One of the pervasive but usually unspoken threats is "doin' more time." Translated, that means if one displeases the authorities, they will influence the Parole Board to lengthen a prisoner's stay beyond the shortest time of one's sentence.

The threats are so subtle and nuanced that prisoners tend to believe that nothing is permitted, or that they dare not risk displeasing the authorities for fear they "get more time." Thus, when Channel

2 came to film the prison, the word among the prisoners was "You can't talk to reporters because it's automatic 'reflection' if you do." But that day, one of the women was angry enough to tell what she thought—tell it into the tape recorder, not before the camera. Prisoners and a matron stood close as she spoke critically of the institution. Afterward, the matron called her aside and advised her not to talk about what she had done with anyone. "The less you say about it, the better it will be for you." The prisoner asked, "Do you mean that someone will 'lay me down' [i.e., some matron would put her in punishment] if I talk about it?" The matron nodded her head.

A short time ago a petition was circulated among prisoners which asked for more liberal visiting policies. Many women agreed with the petition but were afraid to sign for fear they would "get more time."

Most women know that the Director cannot tolerate petitions, views them as a personal attack on her power, and would punish the petitioner more severely than other miscreants. So most would not sign. They were assured of their constitutional right to sign the petition, and if punished, all the signers would take the Director to court. But they refused to sign. Why? Well, all the women had been to court and they knew that there was an approved side and a disapproved side. They knew they were not on the approved side. They doubted that the court would be at all interested in their "constitutional rights."

Another reason was that they *knew* that the laws of this prison were more powerful and would supersede any rights that the Constitution promised them. The law was what the prison personnel said it was. And that was the law that counted. That was the law that would put them in the hole. That was the law that would take away their right to see their friends and family. That was the law that would prolong their time in prison.

Money

Prisoners are paid twenty-five cents a day for working at prison jobs. That's about five dollars a month. Most prisoners must live on that amount. "Live on" means the amount of cigarettes, make-up, pen and pencil, radio batteries, etc., which she can afford to buy at the prison-run Commissary. For she can obtain these items in no other way.

I suppose you would call it a monopoly. And so is the beauty shop. The beauty shop, the Commissary and the laundry are three profit producing areas of the prison.

There is no way a prisoner can get most of the items sold by the Commissary (except as Christmas gifts, for some items) unless she buys them there. The price on most items is only slightly below those of the free world. Cigarettes are 35¢ a pack, 38 sheets of loose-leaf paper filler are 25¢, a bath-sized bar of Dial soap is 25¢, a jar of peanut butter is 45¢, radio batteries are 25¢ apiece. For the month of October 1970, the Commissary showed a profit of well over $2000.00. A jar of *Maxwell House* coffee is $1.25 (the same size costs 99¢ in the free world). *Aqua* net hair spray is 75¢, in the free world it is 50¢.

While the Commissary and Beauty Shop make their profit from the prisoner-as-purchaser, the laundry makes a profit from the prisoner-as-worker.

Where does the profit go?

Why should a profit be made from the pockets of those who have so little?

Why should a profit be made from the prisoner who subsidizes the prison through slave labor?

Laundry

The laundry is not only a money-maker, it is a back-breaker. Until this past Thanksgiving, prisoners worked there on every holiday except Christmas (no one knows why they were allowed freedom from work on that day). The work is physically heavy. One of the more difficult assignments is manually lifting wet (i.e. heavy) linens from one container to another. One job requires guiding a heavy extractor along an overhead track into a floor vat. Sometimes the extractor falls.

Thousands of dirty diapers, coming from the Plymouth State Home, must be processed. Heavy bags and bundles of linens and uniforms must be sorted, piled, lifted and packed. All of these are chores that women must perform. None of the women has sought employment at the laundry. But every day they go to work and wash, iron and pack linens for the prison, for Herman Kiefer Hospital and for Receiving Hospital.

Dietary

If the laundry has the most physically taxing jobs, the dietary work, decentralized to each of seven cottages, requires the greatest tenacity and stamina. When a prisoner is assigned as cook, dishwasher, or dining room girl she works 13 hours a day, seven days a week. There is a respite, however: one day a week is an "easy day." She comes into work at 10:00 a.m. instead of 6:00 a.m. But on that morning she must perform some house cleaning tasks in the cottage where dietary personnel live.

Nor is there such a thing as vacation (for any prisoner!). Women in dietary work around the calendar, and on all holidays—Christmas included.

Consequently, they are more tired and more bored and more angry than any other women "on the court." So some women become subordinate to the matrons. In order to relieve the tedium, some make cookies or small pies. And whenever food is short, the dietary personnel are blamed, even though someone may have stolen food from the kitchen— or the delivery clerk may have brought them short rations.

Because they are so tired and bored, dietary personnel are punished more often than women from any other jobs. Any of the reasons for being consigned to "reflection" are most petty. But reasons for dietary personnel are ridiculous. Sandy, for instance, spent five days in "reflection" for making a cup-cake size pie. Alice spent the same amount of time there for answering a matron with an angry inflection in her voice. One day, three of the five dietary workers from *Cottage 2* went to reflection because someone stole sugar from the kitchen. Two of the five were not put in so that they could produce and clean up after the meals in the cottage. Those selected to go to "reflection" were chosen in the most arbitrary manner. For "the crime" did not relate to personal guilt of dietary personnel, but the sugar thief who might convert his haul into wine. That would be a major disaster.

Pregnant in Prison

When women are imprisoned there is a clear break in the continuity and growth of relationships with their children. It causes personal heartaches that are frequently too heavy for the women to bear. But it does more than destroy their motherhood. Most of the women are of childbearing age. A goodly proportion are pregnant and have their baby in prison. How prison authorities treat the woman and her fetus is instructive. Treatment before and after delivery are seen in the story of Barbara.

She was five and a half months pregnant when she arrived here. Every Tuesday she would go to the prison clinic and have her urine and blood pressure checked. But no one asked any questions or encouraged her to volunteer information about herself. So while she had Rh negative blood, no one at the clinic knew about it. She worked on the cleaning detail—scrubbing floors, lifting trash cans, washing walls—until she delivered. When she was eight months pregnant, she asked the nurse to allow her to change her work to Occupational Therapy. But the nurse said that she would be "better off" working for the entire nine months and refused to o.k. a job transfer.

In her fourth month, Barbara had a kidney problem and her pain was so great that she was sent to an outside hospital. She spent three days there, and passed a kidney stone. She returned to prison with two prescriptions from the "free world doctor." One of these she was not given because the prison clinic personnel did not believe she needed it.

After delivery of the baby at an outside hospital, she returned to prison and was given a job in the Cannery, one month later. At first she peeled tomatoes, but within several days was lifting dishpans full of tomatoes from the steam belt and carrying them ten feet to the conveyor belt. She had to be fast to keep up with the automation. Later, she lifted 100 pound bags of sugar from the floor to a cart, wheeled them to the other side of the building and poured the sugar into large buckets. She lifted the buckets from the floor to a platform higher than the top of her head.

When the baby was two months old, she was assigned the job of cleaning large ketchup bins. In order to get to the bottom, it was necessary to climb up the outside, enter through a door and jump down to the bottom. The floor of the bin was covered with steam coils. One day as Barbara was jumping down to the floor, her bare feet touched the coils which were hot. She was immediately helped out by fellow prisoners and went to the prison clinic. At the clinic her blistered and painful feet were bandaged and she was sent back to the Cannery where the manager assured her he had checked the temperature coils immediately after she went to the clinic, and found them cold. She insisted they were hot—had to be in order to blister her feet. He told her that she was full of bullshit, had manufactured the story to get out of work and was to return to work immediately, bandages and all.

When she was first told about the ketchup bin job, the matron had assured her she wouldn't have to lift sugar packs. But the matron apparently hadn't told the manager, because he forced Barbara to lift the sugar bags since he had made no promises and had to get the work done.

Her experience here was in marked contrast to her other pregnancies in the free world. She never worked before or immediately after those babies were born. She and many other prisoners feel that prison authorities do not believe the women worthy to have children, so work them in contempt for the welfare of mother or baby.

Punishments

As a prisoner, I often wonder what would happen if prison authorities and functionaries did not have the present form of punishment (is it torture?) available to them. If these extremes of human punishment were non-existent, we would have to find more dignified ways of resolving our differences, wouldn't we? For the things which happen in prison punishment sections are evil.

Shirley escaped from prison last summer; she was found and placed in Triple O (which is isolation). She has been there for 3½ months and there is no indication of when, or if, she will be released. Not so long ago, her little girl, whom she hadn't seen in over a year, was brought to prison by the guardian on the regular visiting day. The prison authorities would not allow the visit, even though prisoners are allowed visitors in Triple O. The mother didn't even know her child had come, until she received a note from the guardian a few days later.

Another inmate is in "reflection." She grows
weaker and unsteadier each day. Several prisoners
help the matron walk her to the bathtub. While a
patient in the prison hospital, she broke a window.
She broke the window because no one of the hospital
personnel would take seriously her insistence that
they were giving her the wrong medicine. She had
no visitors to her sick room who could intercede
for her, no personal physician concerned about her
welfare. She was a prisoner in a prison hospital,
treated, not as a patient, but as a prisoner. So breaking that window was both agonized cry and final
plea to take her complaint seriously, and she was
right. They *were* giving her the wrong medication.
But the price she had to pay for being right was ban-
ishment to "reflection."

The most extreme punishment is the Dungeon.
It is a very small cell in the basement of the Administration Building. The floor is concrete; it may or
may not contain a mattress; the prisoner may or
may not be given a blanket and may or may not be
allowed clothing.

The most recent occupant was a mentally ill
woman who was taken there from "reflection." While
in the latter, she got out of her cell several times and
roamed the cottage. She returned to the cell when
offered a cigarette, for that was what she was looking for. On the day she was to see the Discipline
Board (they have the power to free a prisoner from
"reflection") the matron told her they had decided
not to see her. When the prisoner asked why, the
matron replied that the Board hadn't told her why.
The prisoner felt it was a breach of an agreement
made with her earlier, so she began to scream and
pound. But everyone ignored her. Then she turned

the water on in her cell and quietly watched it flood the floor. This produced immediate attention. The guards arrived to take her back to the Dungeon. "I'll be glad to go," she said, "at least I'll get cigarettes there."

There was Silva. She refused to mop the floor, so she was locked in a "reflection" room. That night she began to kick and scream. But no one went to her. Finally she knocked the window out of its setting in the door and the matron called the guards. She struggled and kicked in her desperation so the guards used their fists on her face and body in order to get her into the car. So she rode to the dungeon and there she stayed and screamed. Each day we could hear her scream. Then she began to sing. Then we heard her no longer. Finally they brought this 17 year old girl back to the cottage, a veteran of more than half her years in public institutions. And these institutions have accomplished *what?*

As I write, Theresa, middle-aged, volatile, is being escorted to "reflection." She works in the sewing room. This morning she was given a dress to hem. The matron always marks the place for the hem, but this dress had two marks on it, one an inch higher than the other. Theresa noticed this and put the dress aside so she could check with the matron. But the matron saw it first and insisted that Theresa had made the second mark. The prisoner denied it but was sent to "reflection" anyway. Understand, the hem was not yet in, it would have been placed wherever the matron wanted it. But a woman had to go to the hole!

Finally, there is Louise. She came to prison directly from several hospitalizations in a mental institution. One day she "appeared to be going off."

When this was reported, the officials told the matron to put Louise in Triple O. But she refused to go to Triple O, so they locked her in her room and she spent three weeks there. At first she cried, but later one would never know that she was there.

What is the purpose of this kind of administrative treatment of human beings? How will society ever make restitution to these mistreated fellows? When will society demand an end to 18th century institutions in the midst of the 20th? When will the common man know his guilt, his complicity, in the inhuman treatment of the prisons of his day?

JANE KENNEDY, 44, Chicago; formerly of Trenton, N.J.; graduate of St. Francis Hospital of Nursing (Trenton); BA, MA from University of Pennsylvania; taught at University of Pennsylvania, University of Kentucky, and Loyola University (Chicago); formerly Assistant Director of Nursing for Research and Studies at the University of Chicago Hospitals and Clinics and National Vice-Chairman of the Medical Committee for Human Rights. Convicted, with other members of "Beaver 55," a Catholic anti-war organization, for actions against Dow Chemical Company in Midland, Michigan.

The Impossible Conspiracy at Soledad Prison

Madison Flowers, Jr.

On or about March 18, 1967, a complaint accusing Madison Flowers, Jr. of Statutory Rape was filed in Salano County Municipal Court, city of Vallejo, California, then dismissed at a preliminary hearing, because the complaining Witnesses' statement placed the scene of the Alleged Crime in Napa County, Napa, California. On or about May 9, 1967, the complaint was refiled in Napa County accusing Madison Flowers, Jr. of the same offense, Statutory Rape, in the Napa Municipal Court, and I was present while a preliminary hearing was set for May 22, 1967; I was released after being booked on my own recognizance out of Napa County.

On May 14, 1967, I was apprehended for allegedly receiving stolen property in Salano County, thereafter tried, convicted, and sentenced to six months in the Salano County Jail and three years Felony Probation. While serving the foresaid six months, I was informed on or about the month of November of 1967 that after the six months was up I would be released to the Napa County Sheriff to answer an indictment sent down by the Napa County Grand Jury on June 13, 1967. The indictment handed down on June 13, 1967, accusing Madison Flowers, Jr. of Forcible and Statutory Rape was the same offense pending preliminary hearing in Napa County Municipal Court, May 22, 1967, but the indictment was amended to alleged Forcible Rape as Statutory Rape, while the original complaint of Statutory Rape was still pending preliminary hearing in Napa County Municipal Court. Hereafter, I was tried for Forcible and Statutory Rape in Napa County Superior Court, and convicted of Statutory Rape, and turned over to the California Medical Facilities at Vacaville, California to undergo three months mental evaluation and classification to determine what correctional facility I would serve my time in. While at Vacaville, I filled out an application stating my prior actions, thus the three years felony probation I was given after conviction of allegedly receiving stolen property in Salano County was revoked, and I was given a six-months to ten years sentence to run concurrently with the six months to fifty years sentence that Napa County had given me for Statutory Rape.

On April 22, 1968, I arrived at Soledad North Correctional Training Facility with two sentences running concurrently. Immediately, I ran afoul with the Correctional Officers at North, because at Soledad North there's a three week period in which every new inmate undergoes an orientation as well as a classification period to determine what job assignment, trade, or school level each individual is to begin with or on. During this three week period, an inmate is assigned to miscellaneous jobs, in the Wing, on the yard, or in the Culinary. My objection in regards to the classification system employed is that the officials assign those who need school to the

Culinary, those who need and have the ability for a trade to school, while there are some in trade who need more schooling in order to finish their particular trade assignment, etc. I needed and wanted the school program; instead, the classification committee assigned me to the Culinary. After having worked three weeks in the Culinary, I refused to continue working in the Culinary which caused me to receive ten days C.T.Q. (Confined to Quarters), during which ten days I only came out of my cell to eat; plus I was given thirty days patrol housing, where I wasn't allowed to watch T.V., and if I came in the wing before the yard closed it was only to be locked up. Even after the yard closed I would be locked up on patrol housing.

Prior to reforming, Soledad North Facility was an institution for Y.A.'s (Youth Authority prisoners), and during the process of reforming the officials still employed rules and regulations that originally were to govern Y.A.'s. The inmates from adult institutions find it very hard to adjust to these petty Y.A.'s rules and regulations. Therefore, the inmates who have been in adult institutions in this state and other states find that the continuous harassment of the officials for petty rule infractions is ridiculous, so they seek transfers to adult institutions. Sometimes an inmate will deliberately break a rule that will enable him to receive a transfer.

I personally did eight months of a two year sentence in Cummins Prisons in the State of Arkansas for burglary and grand larceny (eight months is one-third of two years which is the limit to make parole in Arkansas). There you were given a job assignment (mostly in the fields), and you did get or receive an ass whipping for failing to do so. There

was very little harassment from the officials, for each
inmate realized and complied with the seriousness
employed at Cummins Prison, so each did what he
was told without being punished everyday, but of
course there were quite a few ass whippings issued
out to keep the psychological pressure there. But
mostly, it was just physical labor, which was hard
but endurable considering the situation and circum-
stances.

On or about June 2, 1968, I went to the Culinary to eat the evening meal, and the officer assigned
to my wing saw me in line, with my shirt tail out, so
he came over to order me to tuck it in; therefore, I
tucked the shirt in, and mumbled some inaudible
reply. After I had gotten my tray and seated myself,
the officer came over to ask me what did I say
awhile ago, so this was the limit, because he had
been constantly harassing me in and out of the wing,
so I told him to F himself. When I completed the
meal he was waiting for me at the Culinary door to
escort me to Control where I was confined in a holding cell (North Facility utilizes the Adjustment Center at Central, because there's none at North) until
three o'clock in the morning. The officials claimed
that they had forgotten about my being in the holding cell as I trembled from the cold weather. That
morning I was escorted back to the wing only to be
returned to the holding cell three hours later to answer a disciplinary complaint for being disrespectful
to an officer and I received ten days isolation and
escorted to the A.C. at Central.

When I arrived at O-Wing isolation, it was right
after a Black inmate had been fatally stabbed, so I
was cast in the midst of intensified racial chaos. In
isolation I met some of the Brothers who were class-

ified as Militants, and on the official's black list (those to be eliminated because of their degree of political awareness and affiliation in Militant or racial type groups within the institution).

These Brothers attempted to enlighten me on the tyrannism imposed by the officials against Black inmates, but I thought they were prevaricating, because the stories they conveyed to me seemed utterly impossible. They told me about Black inmates being stabbed, being tear-gassed in cells with little or no ventilation; of Black inmates being put on exercises with nine and ten inmates of other ethnic groups for the purpose of eliminating the lone Black inmate. They told me of officials giving inmates of other ethnic groups weapons to use on Black inmates. Again, I thought impossible.

After associating with these Brothers they told me that the officials would automatically classify me in the Militant category, and to be aware, because I would surely be put on an exercise to be eliminated, but at the time I was completely unaware of what this Militant label really meant. So after my ten days isolation were up, and the officials from North came to escort me back to North Facility, I refused to go back in favor of going to Central Main-line, but the officials assigned me to O-Wing to wait for my transfer papers to be filled out.

After moving from O-One to O-Two (first and second tiers in O-Wing), I began to believe the truth the Brothers in isolation told, i.e. partially, because when I came in O-Two the inmates of other ethnic groups began to say they brought us some more nigger meat in as they chanted a "Nigger Song." The officials made no effort to impede this chaotic scene, so I thought if I minded my own business I would be going to the main line soon, but this didn't work, because about three days later I was washing my face to come out for breakfast (you come out of your cell to receive your breakfast and evening meals then return to it to eat the meal), and a Spanish-American inmate working as porter came to my cell and asked if I knew the Brothers in isolation, so I said yes, why? Then he stated that he would kill me when we came out to exercise. I had had enough of their Nigger singing and harrassment so I spit in his face, and told him he better, because I would be out.

When we came out to exercise this same inmate approached me with his hand in his pocket, so I advanced toward him about five feet away and he stopped, and began telling me to proceed to the back of the tier where we would fight. I started toward the back with him on one side of the tier and I on the other side. Half the distance of the tier I looked over my shoulder and there were four of his friends preceding us; here, I stopped while friends of mine asked what was happening. I gave them a brief statement of what had transpired; therefore they told the guy to go on and fight me head-up, but he was reluctant even though he had a weapon, and knew I couldn't possibly have one when there was no way for Black inmates to obtain weapons. At the time I had a sock with my earphones stuffed in it. We stood there talking until the officials saw that nothing would occur, so the officials ordered us to lock up, then they moved some Black inmates, they said for agitating, to Max-Row and isolation. I think they moved two Spanish American inmates, but only as a camouflage.

The officials put me on cell exercise for two days, they claimed, while they investigated the incident. I came out on the third morning to receive my break-fast meal, and I was the only Black out of seven or eight from the other ethnic groups; then a white inmate swung at me with his fist. I ducked the blow, and hit him with my tray; thus we fought until the officials shot gas on us. Thereafter, I was taken to the Committee and given fifteen days isolation and assigned to Max-Row for ninety days.

On Max-Row I was back with the Blacks I met when I first came in A.C. Here again they told me not to go to sleep during the day, because the officials had given the other ethnic groups zip-guns to shoot Blacks, and not to drink any milk or coffee, because it was full of cleanser, urine, feces, etc. This time I paid close attention and somehow we obtained a mirror, and the Brothers gave me the mirror because I was murmuring about not being able to drink milk. To stop my murmuring they gave me the mirror and told me to watch as the porter passed out the coffee and milk. As I watched I saw the guys in the cell before us pour liquid substances into the pitchers of coffee and milk. Then one day a white inmate shot at a Black inmate next door to me, so I became a true believer after seeing him shoot at the Brother next door.

At this time there were inmates from each ethnic group who wouldn't do much racial talk, because most of these inmates had been down for awhile, and knew how to conduct themselves. The Black inmates wrote up a petition to get more canteen, because at that time we were only allowed cosmetics, tobacco, and coffee out of the canteen. The petition also re-quired a Black porter to be put out, and better food, but the officials didn't do anything until we started throwing feces and urine on them. Then they added a few items to the canteen list and put a Black porter out, but the food remained repetitious.

After the melee the officials moved all but four Blacks off Max-Row. This is the theory the officials work on: if a Black shows any potential leadership ability he is detrimental to them, and most Black inmates confined in A.C. are self-educated, because the officials will not let them stay on any main line long enough to acquire any education, so they read pocket books in A.C. and obtain a 50,000 word dictionary, and those who are righteously sincere in learning do learn. All these facts contribute to Black inmates being denied parole year after year: political awareness from self-education, leadership and their degree of involvement in revolutionary groups in the institution is frowned upon, and their prison record has little or no connection with these parole denials. Impossible? No, very possible, in fact, true!

The officials eventually manipulated me in a position where I would be injured or murdered. I had an altercation with an officer working on Max-Row, so during this time they were giving me various petty one-fifteens to keep me on Max-Row. After I had this altercation with this officer, they had three Blacks on Max-Row. I was the only one eligible for the porter job since the officials had framed the other Blacks by putting knives in their cells during the search procedure. In fact, this officer whom I had an altercation with claimed that he found five knives in one Black's cell at various times. The reason for this was that this particular Black only had a five year sentence so with his awareness he was considered detrimental to society; thus the officials had to scheme to give him more time, which they did, a three year to life sentence. This officer gave me the porter's job, then three or four days later deliberately left another inmate's door open while I was supposed to be the only one out; therefore, I was stabbed in the left hand, and sent to the isolation strip cells. For what? Also, utterly nothing, because when the guy attacked me I caught the first blow in the left hand, and stepped back in my cell; there was no defense for me, so I accepted the defeat.

After this incident they chanted coward Nigger for sixty days, then the Committee sent me to X-Wing to do a sixty day program. X-Wing is where I met W. L. Nolen (one of the Black inmates killed on January 13, 1970, and at this time he was programming, but still didn't get any consideration from the program committee to be released to the main line). The last part of October 1968, two white inmates attacked W. L. Nolen with steel pipes right in view of the gun tower, and the officer in the gun tower shot the warning shot and W. L. stopped fighting. From what W. L. told me the officials had tried to get inmates to kill him before this incident, but he had trained himself to respond quickly, thus countering all prior attempts on his life, yet, the officials wanted him eliminated because he had everything they considered detrimental to them and society which I reiterate: political awareness, leadership ability, self-education, and involvement in groups for the betterment of the inmates. There's one thing clear in every Black inmate's mind who was in X-Wing when this occurred, the officials gave those pipes to the white inmates. There were actually three inmates in the attack, but one had a prison-made knife and that's when the fight started. To begin with they sneaked up on W. L. from behind and hit him in the back of the head, which had only gotten him angry.

The officials sent W. L. to isolation for being attacked, and three or four days later they sent Howard Tole and myself to isolation. Howard went on general principles, and I went for allegedly stabbing a white inmate. So there we were, studying religious material, and wondering what form of conspiracy they had planned next. We all had twenty-nine days isolation so after nine days the officials asked Howard and me if we wanted to go to Max-Row. After deliberating on this we thought the officials had something planned for us in Max-Row, but nothing occurred until two days later. W. L. came out to exercise, then was assigned to walk alone, and then the officials had left a white inmate's door open. Max-Row and isolation is back to back, so we heard the officer shouting "lock up, Nolen! lock up!" When W. L. finally came to Max-Row he told Howard and myself that the officer left a white inmate's door open and he had a knife but he (W. L.) kicked him and in turn the white inmate ran back to his cell.

Edward (also one of the Black inmates killed January 13, 1970), came to isolation, and the same incident occured with him, but Edward knocked the white inmate out, so then officials sent him to the Max-Row also. Right after Edward came over, the officials transferred Howard to Folsom Prison.

This time I stayed on Max-Row for eight months while the white inmates chanted Nigger Songs all day and night. Everyday the white inmates would either shoot at or throw feces and urine on the Black inmates.

During this time W. L. was working as porter

and three times the officer left a white inmate's door open (Max-Row was segregated) and the white inmates refused to come out, since they knew W. L., but yet these inmates would sing that nigger song and throw feces and urine on W. L. Once the officer had the bar set on-key when W. L.'s door was open, but on-key W. L. couldn't open the door. The officer came down and keyed a cell's door to bring in an inmate; then after the inmate was in the officer locked it with the key, but he claimed he forgot to give the white inmate a mattress. When he brought the mattress down and went back to the front and rolled the bar, this automatically enabled W. L. to come out with the white inmate. So he came out running toward the white inmate, but he was too slow because the white inmate had beat a fast retreat to his cell.

For months after months the whites tried to devastate every Black on Max-Row when the exercise opened. The officials kept stating that the yard would open soon, so even though I had had no write-ups and was eligible to go to X-Wing, I stayed on Max-Row waiting for the yard to open. Finally after waiting a period of time, I went to X-Wing to do a program. First I was assigned to the first tier under the supervision of gun tower for thirty days; then to the second tier where I stayed two days, because on the third day I went to the exercise yard with two other Blacks and nine mixed other ethnic groups. The officials searched each individual but after the exercise period was just about up, two white inmates came at me with prison-made knives. I was stabbed seven or eight times while the officer blew his whistle, but each wound was only superficial, due to my agileness in rolling with each hit.

Again every Black knew what was happening. But who would believe this impossible conspiracy? If we wrote to tell our families or friends the officials would only return the letter citing that no one was trying to do anything to the Black who wrote the letter.

After I was attacked and stabbed the officials placed me on the first tier on cell exercise, until they investigated the incident. Five days later I went to the Committee, and they stated they were still investigating the incident. So on my return from the Committee room, I stopped to obtain some books from a friend of mine, and the officer escorting me back to my cell prevaricated in saying he overheard me ask for a knife, and that I refused to be locked. There was a mixed group on the tier exercising, so the officials said that I was trying to acquire a knife to use on one of the white inmates. While I was out, the gun tower officer was standing with the 30-30 pointed in my direction. But the truth was that the officials had to find justification for keeping me under the supervision of the gun tower, therefore they fabricated a justification.

I kept a clean record from November 3, 1969 until May 20, 1970 so the officials couldn't find any justification for confining me to A.C. any longer. May 20, 1970, I went back to North Facility only to be faced with that working in the Culinary thing again. After going through the orientation and classification routine again, I asked to be placed in the welding shop, but the officials stated that I had mis complied my I.Q., therefore I would have to go to school. I went to school, and one week later the school officials said that I had a ten point four average when the welding only required an eight poin even. Now, the officials told me that the welding trade list was so long until it would take me two years to get into welding. Therefore, I asked for typing in the afternoon which they gave their approval of, but the next day I received a write-up for refusing to work in the Culinary. At the noon meal I was called to work in the Culinary, so I knew the officials had made a mistake. Therefore I went to Control and elucidated the situation to the assignment lieutenant, whereas he informed me that I had been dropped from the school which automatically caused me to be assigned back to Culinary. I asked the lieutenant to call the educational department, which he did, and they informed him that I was supposed to be in afternoon school, but they had misplaced the papers transferring me from morning school to afternoon. The lieutenant told me to go on and work in the Culinary, that I would be back in school the next day. Therefore I complied with this. During the noon meal the lieutenant came in and talked with me as I served the noon meal. The next day I was called to answer a disciplinary complaint; as I walked toward control I was wondering what could it possibly be (the disciplinary complaint). When I got to control I was face to face with one of the racist officers at North, Sergeant Smith substituting as lieutenant that day. The write-up stated that I refused to show up for work in the Culinary, so I went to the other lieutenant who had talked to me as I worked and he refrained from answering. Again I received ten days C.T.Q. but that day the officials changed tactics. This time they alleged that I assaulted an officer in order to be transferred out of North. The reason the officials wanted me out of North Facility is that I was teaching awareness to those who would listen and the things I taught were all facts the listeners knew.

Back in O-Wing I heard "bang bang bang three dead Niggers." Again the feces and urine treatment, but this time the officials changed Program Administrators, and the five Blacks on Max-Row asked for an integrated exercise; the P.A. compromised by putting a black and white porter out. Three days before this the officials stood up front shouting Lock Up! as the white inmates threw feces and urine on the Black inmates. Here the officials knew that the porters would fight, so they had given the white inmate a knife which he was afraid to use after he was out with the Black porter. As the two porters stood talking the officials also looked on. When they realized that the white inmate couldn't entice Satch into attacking him by calling Satch various nigger names, they ordered the two porters to Lock Up. Then came my turn to come out with a white inmate; immediately the white swung hitting me on the upper part of my head. But there was no wire for him, I whipped him until the officials shot tear gas on me, then took me to a strip cell for two days. In the Committee room I told the officers to give me the same thing they had given the white inmate which was nothing, so I got nothing for the write-up.

The officials quickly dissolved Max-Row and sent the inmates confined there to either upper O Wing or X-Wing. X-Wing is where I'm presently at and after clean time here (without disciplinary complaint) the officials still refused to give me any consideration going to the main line. Once they put me up for transfer to San Quentin, which was denied, then they put me up for transfer to San Quentin again, but I knew that I would only be denied

Therefore I asked to be transferred to Chino Palm Adjustment Center to do ninety days to either go to Chino mainline or else transferred to C.M.C. main line.

Instead of progressing they have the inmates retrogressing. Instead of rehabilitation they have the inmates deteriorating. Every time the inmates start functioning for the betterment of all the inmates, the officials speak of racial confusion to take the pressure off themselves which we, the inmates as a whole, had applied.

Presently I'm going to court for again allegedly assaulting an officer with force likely to produce great bodily harm. The outcome of this can be stated with certainty. I will receive a three years to life sentence, because there is no impartial justice here. Even if I'm found innocent, the parole committee will only deny me parole year after year until they think they have broken my spirit of awareness, so I will be in prison for quite awhile since I will not succumb.

I really should not complain because, after all, these officials have tried to have me murdered twice, allowed feces and urine to be placed in my food and thrown on me; locked me up for twenty-three-and-a-half hours a day and recently seven days a week with only twenty minutes out to shower on Sunday; come to my cell, put a belt around me with handcuffs attached, and while I stand on the tier in my underwear and socks, shackled down, they allow two white inmates to kick me; when I move to retaliate they kindly throw me down and stand on me, while one busts my head, two twist my feet, but yet I should not complain.

Mail for me stops in the Program Administrator

Office. He decided that if I can receive mail, I wil
receive letters two and three weeks old, but yet I
deserve this because I'm Black, and trying to do my
time. But as the officials say, "We don't like no
smart Nigger." By this they mean an intelligent
Black Man who, through his intelligence, is drawing
other Blacks to listen to him. The officials had over-
estimated my intelligence, like I mostly function on
what being in this environment has taught me.

Memories of Danbury

J. R. (Bob) Jones

The Berrigan brothers got to Danbury a few months after I was released. I'm sorry I missed them. It might have been interesting for us all. But I do remember reading in the papers where one of them —I think it was Father Phillip—referred to Danbury as a "popsicle prison."

The term I heard used was "country club." Everybody seemed to agree that Federal Correctional Institution, Danbury was the "country club" of the federal prison system. Maybe so. I had never pulled time in any other prison, and for that matter never belonged to a country club. So I wouldn't know.

But I did nine months and sixteen days at Danbury for contempt of Congress—the House Un-American Activities Committee wanted me to rattle off the names of my Klan-people, and I pleaded the Fifth, which didn't stand up because I was an officer of a registered corporation—and whatever you call it, popsicle prison or country club, it isn't fun and it isn't easy. Maybe it's not supposed to be.

I remember just before my sentencing date with the judge, the Department of Justice sent some guy to the house. He came in with his suit and his attache

case. And he had a deal for me. If I would resign
from the United Klans and denounce that organization, he'd see to it that the judge gave me a sus-
pended sentence and not even any fine.

I told him: "My soul wasn't for sale in 1965.
What makes you think my soul is for sale now?"

He said: "Mr. Jones, 240 days behind bars is a
long, *long* time."

I said: "I can wrestle a damn bear in a bathtub
for 240 days! Now, git!"

And after Syble talked to him even more vigorously, he did *git*. I don't consider I "threatened"
that particular federal officer. I think I was just telling him—rather forcefully, I admit—that he wasn't
welcome.

I actually served 291 days, but at that time I
had no idea whether the judge was going to give me
one year to do, or five, or something in between. I
don't know how that guy from the Department of
Justice knew, but he did. Makes you wonder, doesn't
it?

I was real bitter at first. I came back to North
Carolina and muttered that they owed me nine
months and sixteen days. I wasn't at all sure how
I was going to collect on that debt, but I was sure
they owed it to me. Well, as everybody knows, bitterness or hate generally destroys the man who's got
it. I got over my bitterness, and tried instead to learn
some things from the experience about myself and
my country. So here's some of what I learned.

I heard the big steel doors clank behind me for
the first time on March 28, 1969, at 5:05 p.m. I
was at FCI Danbury, Conn., and when you hear
those steel doors slam for the first time you think

your heart is going to fall out through the soles of
your orthopedic shoes.

They left me alone for a few minutes in a little
room off to the side. I guess the U.S. Marshals
who brought me in were getting the body receipt
signed by the authorities at Danbury. I prayed a lot
in those first few minutes, and I thought about Syble
and Sheila (my wife and daughter), and thousands
of Klans-people I know, and these thoughts did sustain me.

I'd been there about five minutes, when the door
opened and a man walked in and stuck out his hand.

"Mr. Jones," he said, "I'm Frank Kenton, the
Warden here. And the one thing you'll have to remember is that you're a resident of Connecticut
now."

I stood up and shook his hand. But I told him:

"You're crazier than hell, Mister! I'm a resident
of North Carolina! I'm a *convict* in Connecticut!"

After Warden Kenton and I had our little con-
versation, he left the room and I went into the A/O
Section (Admission/Orientation) for two weeks,
which is what happens to every prisoner.

Later that same night, over in the A/O building,
I talked with my first guard. He was an old black
man. [In my own mind, I make distinctions between
black guys, colored guys and "niggers"—who are
found in all races.] Anyway, this black man had
been in the federal prison system for twenty-nine
years. Matter of fact, he retired while I was at Danbury, and on his last night he came by my cell to
say good-bye. I wished him luck; he was a fine old
man, and he told me: "Bob, you're the first Klans-
man I ever met. But of course I've been reading about
the Klan all my life. If they're all like you, maybe

we can work it out without killing each other."

I told him, *that's right.* And I also told him we
had a lot of *fine* young Klans-people coming up in
North Carolina, who are a lot smarter and better
educated than I'll ever be.

But on this first night in the A/O building, this
old black guard was just sitting there at a desk chew-
ing on a half-lit cigar. He took my folder, glanced
at it, and said:

"Contempt of *Congress?* What the hell *is that?*
I been in this man's prison system for twenty-nine
years, and I never heard of such a thing!"

I said, "Neither have I. But I reckon I *do* have
a lot of contempt for Congress these days."

He said: "Jones, what do you do on the outside?"

And I said: "Since 1963, I've been the elected
head of the Ku Klux in North Carolina."

He almost swallowed his cigar. But then he got
me something to eat and a bunk and got me settled.
I was "home" for the next nine months and 16 days.

The prisoners came in all shapes and sizes at
Danbury. The prison had a rated capacity of 400
and the day I left there were 716 inmates so you
can understand how crowded it all was. We had
about 180 drug addicts in the prison population,
four of whom died of overdoses while I was there.
It later turned out they were getting the stuff from
a guy who worked in the dispensary for the doctor.
And I think they caught him by running a couple of
FBI agents, posing as prisoners, into Danbury.

We had maybe 200 fags. They were a nicely
"integrated" group of whites, blacks and Puerto
Ricans, and they were pretty much kept "segregated"
from the rest of the prison. I was put into their build-

ng for a few days because there was no other place for me. They didn't mess with me and I didn't mess with them. They called me *Mister* Jones. But I must say I was glad to get out of their building.

We also had twenty-three draft-card burners. As nearly as I could make out, twenty-two of them were Jews and one was a nigger—and he was part-Jewish. This group had some other things in common which interested me. They were all very intelligent and had a lot of schooling under their belts. They all had some college and most had finished and had done some graduate work. They had messed around with drugs. I never became friends with any of them (they're not my type), but we were acquaintances, and we talked out in the yard, sometimes. I'm bothered when I think that the smartest and best-trained people hate the country and its government so much that they will burn their draft cards and go off to jail for it.

My pinochle partner was in for murder, and just as nice a guy as you'd ever want to meet. He'd gotten involved in a barroom brawl in Alaska, when the state was still a territory, and when the brawl was over there was a cat laying dead on the floor. So my pinochle partner had already served about twenty years, and he had another twelve to go.

We even had a black interstate rustler! This guy explained to me one day how he did it. "Bob, it's simple. These big farmers in Arkansas are all Christians, and they go off to Sunday School and Church every Sunday. So I find what time they cut out for Church, and I roll in my truck. I got at least an hour to load up some of their prize cattle and high-tail it across the bridge into Memphis before they get back!"

So I laughed and told this cat what they used to
do to rustlers in the Old West, regardless of their
race, creed or color. And on Christmas morning
when he was playing some of his music too long and
too loud, I thought we were all going to string him
up right there. But we didn't, of course. We just
scared him half to death talking about it.

We had fourteen other prisoners from North
Carolina at Danbury. Two of them were black guys
and one was a nigger. Most of them were behind
walls for making moonshine liquor. It's the only
trade they know, and as soon as they get out they
go right back to it. Several of them are out now
and they've asked me to get them a job or loan
them some money, to get them out of some little
drunk tank somewhere. And I did.

Speaking of the North Carolina contingent, I
should add something here. Granite Quarry, North
Carolina, where I live, is 814 miles from Danbury.
We clocked it. But I was lucky. One of my good
Klans-people is a fine pilot, and once a month he'd
crank up his airplane and fly Syble and Sheila up to
Connecticut for two hours of precious visiting time.
But the other North Carolinians didn't have anything like that going for them, and they'd be lucky
to get two visits a year from their family. I think the
federal prison system tries its best to assign a man
to the prison nearest his home, but in many cases
that just isn't possible.

I should mention a black prisoner named Bob
Young. He was a good fellow, who came down a
hard road in New England somewhere. Bob was an
ex-prizefighter, and at one time was a ranking light
heavyweight. But he never quite made it. You know
what happens to ex-prizefighters who don't quite

make it? This one held up a bank. And he did it in a real dumb way and got caught. Bob Young had some mental illness problems, and he didn't have friend-one on the outside. He tried to be friendly with everybody on the inside, including me. Most of the black prisoners hated him for it. They regarded him as a "white man's nigger" or an "Uncle Tom." Every now and then there would be an incident where the hatred the other black prisoners felt for Bob Young would combine with his mental problems, and *bam-bam!* Bob would throw a couple of punches and there would be some cat knocked cold on the floor. The more hatred I see, the sadder I feel.

There were a couple of bad ones in Danbury, and I use the words advisedly. They were always mouthing off about "getting the Dragon." Back in North Carolina, I wouldn't pay any attention to talk like that. On my home turf, my security arrangements are very good. Not perfect, but good. But in prison, you have to perk up an ear when somebody starts talking like that. So I mentioned it to Syble on one of her visits, and she mentioned it to a friend of ours on the outside, Pete Young (no relation to Bob Young; Pete is white, at least most of the time), and Pete made a couple of phone calls to some Muslim ministers he knows. They were Sunni Muslims, not the "Black Muslims" of Elijah Muhammed. In fact, after Malcolm X had split with Elijah, Malcolm went over to these Sunni orthodox Muslims, and they taught him, and eventually buried him. I didn't know any of this at the time. All I knew was that these two Muslim ministers and their assistants and bodyguards suddenly showed up one day at Danbury to hold a prayer service for the black prisoners. Bob Young slipped me the word to be waiting out-

side the chapel for these Muslim ministers, and
did. And we had a very good talk for about fifteen
or twenty minutes, until the Warden came by and
saw the Dragon talking with the robed Muslim min
isters. I swear I saw his knees buckle. The Muslim
also slipped out a word or two. They passed the
word that if anything happened to the Dragon, they
were "off the planet."

End of trouble. And I appreciated it. Those
Muslims risked their leadership positions with their
own people to help me out. And they did so, I think
because they know these last few years have been
very difficult for all North Carolinians, white and
black, and that the state has come close on several
occasions to a nasty little race war. They also know
that my Klans-people have been a powerful force in
North Carolina for keeping the lid on and thereby
saving a lot of lives of various colors. So the Mus
lims made a courageous gesture of friendship, and
perhaps some day the situation will be reversed and
I will reciprocate.

The guards? Most of them were fine men. A few
of them abused their position, and were not re
spected by either their fellow guards or the inmates
My last night in Danbury, I had seven of the guards
on the night shift come by my cell and ask would
be all right to look me up if they ever passed through
North Carolina. Two of them have already done so
and they sat in my living room with their wives and
children, and we had a couple of drinks and laughed
and told Danbury stories.

And then there were the administrators. Warden
Kenton, the Associate Warden, Dixie Walker, a
Southern boy, and, of course, my caseworker, a
black named Mayberry. He took a lot of pleasure

in messing with me; he enjoyed being in the catbird seat, and he let me know it. I let him know that he should pass through North Carolina quickly en route to Florida or wherever he happened to be going.

So what does it all mean? If I knew what was wrong with the country or how to cure it, I'd write a book. Or maybe tell the President. Our Wizard, Bobby Shelton, who also pulled nine-months-plus for "contempt," sometimes says: "There are a lot of things I don't understand, and a lot of things I *mis*understand. But there are a few things I *do* understand."

I understand that not all those who talk about heaven are going there. And not all those who claim to be *political* prisoners are. A cat holds up a gas station or a liquor store, and then when he gets to jail he spends some time with one of those draft-card-burner types, who runs it down for him, and the cat says, "Hey, great! I'm a political prisoner!" *Bull!* He's a stickup man.

Prison reform? Sure, I'm for it. Start by paying a decent wage to the guards and other prison personnel. Start by making a law that *every* judge in America has to serve thirty days in a prison before he can get on the bench and send others away. A guy asked me the other day if I was in favor of prisoners having overnight visits from their wives and girlfriends. Well, I damn sure was in favor of it when *I* was in jail. But given the way things are now, there would be a lot of practical problems involved in something like that.

Mail? Of course a prisoner's mail has to be inspected for contraband—weapons and dope. But my mail was constantly messed with at Danbury, over such things as stories from the *New York*

Times that people like Pete Young were sending me. As they say in the military, there *is* a difference between being tough and being chickenshit. From my limited experience, I can guess that our prisons are *not* tough, and *are* chickenshit. As with so many things in this country, we've got it exactly bass ackwards.

Can a poor man get justice in America? My answer will surprise you. My answer is, yes. The poor men I knew in jail were guilty as hell, and admitted it. The problem is not that poor people in America *don't* get justice. The problem is that rich people *evade* justice. Think about *that!* Justice for the rich man ought to be just as swift and certain as it usually is for the poor man. And it isn't.

Was *I* a political prisoner? Sure, and there were some others in Danbury when I was there, notably the one-time mayor of a small town in New Hampshire, who bucked his state's political machine and got five long *years* for being $240 behind on his taxes. Just because everybody claims to be a political prisoner doesn't mean that nobody is a political prisoner.

The federal government tried everything they knew to break the Klan in North Carolina. We must have embarrassed them something fierce. Agents visited the employers of many of my Klans-people and got them fired. Somebody—I wouldn't know who, but I don't think it was blacks—arranged for anonymous, threatening phone calls and letters to Klans-people. Our units were heavily infiltrated by pathetic informers, who badly needed the money that various police agencies waved under their noses. My state officers were tailed everywhere they went and "leaned on." ("Hey, boy, when you gonna get smart and get out of the Klan and tell us what you know.")

And did all of this hurt us? I never would answer that question before, but I'll answer it now. *It damn sure did.* Many of my Klans-people got scared out, and I can't find it in my heart to blame them. You think there were times when I wasn't scared? And another bunch got confused and discouraged and ran off to the woods to form little splinter "Klan" groups that (they think) will someday blow up the world.

Yes, we got hurt. We got hurt *bad*. When the dust settled, we found that we had gotten slimmed down to the *third* bunch of Klans-people, whose heads are on so securely that the federal government will never be able to touch them. So now it's a Mexican standoff, and we are coming back slowly from our losses of the last few years. I don't mean to brag, and one must be careful about predicting such things, but I *think* we won.

And we have slowly and painfully learned that it is necessary to approach many different kinds of people with (1) respect and (2) cautious friendship. All Americans—not just Klans-people—have been poisoned with hate for years. Pray God that we all have vomited most of that hatred up and out of our systems.

So I pulled a short bit at Danbury. Even if it was short, I don't think I could have made it without faith in my God, my wife and daughter, the surviving Klans-people in North Carolina, various friends, and fellow inmates and guards.

Black Students Released from Parchman

CHARLESTON, Miss. — Approximately 125 black students, arrested here yesterday for trespassing and disturbing the peace, were released early today from the State Penitentiary at Parchman. The prisoners had been taken to Parchman in school buses because "there wasn't enough room for all of them in Charleston," according to the assistant superintendent at the State Penitentiary. They were released on their own recognizance about 1 A.M. today, but no date for a hearing has been set.

The prisoners, ranging from the seventh to the twelfth grades, were among those involved in a boycott of Allen Carver High School which began last Friday. "If you take one of us, you must take all of us," they were reported to have told the police. The boycott was in protest of the court-approved plan which permitted both black and white students to be bused between the two high schools several times a day. Mrs. Lucy Boyd, chairman of the Tallahatchie County chapter of the National Association for the Advancement of Colored People, insisted that the black students "couldn't have been trespassing on school property" when they were arrested. "They were outside the fence, not on school property." Mrs. Boyd announced that the boycott will continue.

Sheriff Dogan had to obtain a court order to permit him to take the prisoners to the State Penitentiary at Parchman, 32 miles away. Some of the female prisoners had to help in the kitchen to prepare food at the penitentiary before they were released early this morning. They were returned to Charleston in school buses.

Oct 26 1970

On Tuesday morning
we were lining up and the
Leader said get a stragh line
and then the offical came
and said you are under arrest
and we said if you take one
you must take all so then
he said Get to buses and they said
bus up. So we got on the bus.
and they pull of. When we got
a little peace of the said that
we are going to parchman.
then when we got ~~near~~ near there
the place the man got a said a
few words. And when we got
to parchman they serach us.
and took us to the cell. And
they brought some food and
when serving the food they
took four girls and told them
to cook the food was half
done and the man serve
with his hand. And then
the came back with some
food to sell. we bought some

74

thing. About 10:00 they came with some half done ham brugers, then they came with some pillows and sheets blankets. Ont mattress. then we went to bed and 12 oclock we were laughing they came and say let's go so they got 4 at a time and they let boys went o none bus. Girl on another bus other wise we were fine and when we got half way home the bus paddle on the ~~car~~ celerator ~~got~~ ~~tea~~ stuck and a girl had to pull it up. And then she said you dam folks are almost home. When when got to charleston we went to Saint Paul church ond thats all.

Sherry A. Jones, 11 years old
404 So. Franklin St.
Charleston, Miss. 38921

Oct. 21 ATD

On Tuesday morning We Were linning
Up in fort of the School. And One of
the officil Came and Said you Are Undr
Arrest And So We got on the Bus And on
Our way We Song freedom Song And the
Bus Slowed down a while And We all
throught that they Slowed down to make
Us Pick Cotton, But the bus Star bact
to going and We Start Our Freedom Son
again.

~~Now~~ We get to Parahman and
We Stop At gate and one man said We
got Some dam nigger I don't know who
the man was, And it Was about a half Of
An hour ~~befo~~ before We got Of the Bus
And When they did a let Us off it was
half way raining.

~~Now the food or what~~

~~And~~ After We got on the inside
We Were Serche and given our names
and Address and Parnets names als
So We went into the ~~se~~ Cell thdre We
and matbresses, ~~col~~ Sheets, Pillows, nor
blankets or in other words the Beds

were tin and it had rust on them and and
and we were tire. When we got there
So we had to lay down on those hard
dry beds and some girls used thire coats
for protection on those hard beds.
Now the food they had some trustees
to sever our food one man put his hands
in the greens and throught them on our
plates and they made four girls go out
and help cook the food. And they also
gave us two old musty winners and
something they call tea.

And about four hour later they came
to sell. Some, Cand, Gum, Cigarettes and that all. And about
four hours later they came back with
two slices of bread with half dona
hamburges in it and some tea.

And abut three hours later they
came and said get up four girls at a
time. And went and sign our names
again out and we got on the bus
and we were on our way home again.

Mary L. Johnson
504 So. Franklin St.
Charleston, Miss 38921

77

Dear Joyce

Albert Johnson

The following is a brief, but precise evaluation of my past life as a so-called citizen and ex-convict of the Department of Corrections of one of our largest states, a prison system that does everything excluding what its name implies, which I think that you, too, will agree with upon completion of this letter.

I was born in Chicago, the sixth of seven children in August, 1927. My mother and father separated when I was five years old, and although I never knew what fatherly love was because my father never had time to show it, I felt the emptiness that was caused by my parents' separation and two years later when I was only 7 years old, I experienced pain and grief at its utmost, for that was when my mother died. My grandmother and eldest sister did their best toward making a living for us, which was a hard struggle for them due to lack of experience and education, which is a problem of black people even now in present-day times. I had within me a desire to break away from this thing that had suppressed me and my family for so long. As time passed, I realized that this was almost impossible, for I was up against a giant and by having no weapons so to speak, I was powerless, but none-theless, there remained in me hope and most of all determination.

I came to this state at the age of 15, hoboing around simply for survival and as I think about it now, I was like an animal in the jungle, surviving nature as best as he could, but like the wild jungle, the asphalt jungle had its enemies and I was to find out all too soon that I was at their mercy, not be-cause I wanted to, but because I was yet powerless, and thus fell prey to the mighty giant, whose clutches pressed into me a hate for it and all it stood for. This hate all but diminished me.

My final personal encounter with this mighty giant was in the form of the law. I had been fortu-nate by gaining employment at the shipyards and had acquired a little money and a car. I had a long-ing to visit my family, who at that time had moved to this same state. Since I was driving, I stopped over in the big city and checked into a hotel to rest up for the remainder of the trip. While there, I came into contact with an associate and his female com-panion, who expressed a desire to show me the town. It was while we were driving around that we picked up a third passenger, a merchant seaman flashing a large sum of money. What happened next, I was unaware of until I was stopped by a policeman and arrested for robbery. I later found out that the fe-male who was riding with me had propositioned the merchant seaman. He accepted her proposition, but during the process, she had slipped a knock-out drop in one of his drinks and released him of all his money. Since they were all passengers in my car, the law automatically involved me as part of the crime, and I was found guilty of Grand Theft and sent to the reformatory as a Juvenile Authority commitment.

This was in 1946, the beginning of my hell and undiminished hate. While at the reformatory, I had built up in me a resentment toward authority resulting from the assaults made upon me from the very beginning of my arrest. The arresting officer had hit me across my head with his revolver and called me names, such as "You're one of those smart niggers," when I asked why had he stopped me. I was always pushed or shoved whenever I was in chow lines, as a number of other blacks were also being treated, but I had noticed that the white population were just asked to move along. I regarded myself as a man and resented being treated like a child. I expressed these thoughts one day as I was being pushed forcefully by an officer while I was in chow line, whereas a fight started between the officer and me, provoked by the officer himself. Six other brothers and several officers were also involved. Resulting from this altercation, I was labeled as an instigator, trouble-maker and declared unsuitable to the environment of the youth reformatory, whereas I was transferred to one of this state's famous Maximum Securty prisons. I was still under a Juvenile Authority commitment, because I had been before no judge or court whatsoever.

Upon my arrival to the pen I was subjected to an even greater hell. While in the pen I was assigned to the furniture shop in which I received constant harrassment. I was surrounded by Adult Commitments, and since I was the only J.A. in the furniture shop, I kept mostly to myself. Most of the cons I worked with were informers, uncle toms, etc. And the officer in charge of the shop had these cons to constantly prod me. One day three of these cons needled me into a fight and to even the odds, I grabbed an iron pipe and whipped one of them almost to death with it. This caused another black mark against me, for I was placed in isolation for 29 days, then placed in segregation while going to court on a charge of ADW (Assault with a Deadly Weapon). I was sentenced to 1-10 years, as an Adult Commitment with the number A-6158, which I still possess today. Subsequently, I was released on parole in 1949 to the custody of my sister who lived in this state.

During the few months that I was out of prison, I realized with shocking reality what it meant to be a marked man. Actually, there were three marks against me, being poor, black and ex-con. Although I had learned a trade in prison, I found it extremely difficult to find employment and I knew that I was an extra burden on my sister, for her husband was struggling hard enough trying to provide for his wife and three children. Eventually I found several small paying jobs such as porter, dishwasher, etc. but none of them ever lasted longer than a week or two because they would find out that I was an ex-con, thus finding me untrustworthy and out of a job, and finally back in the pen, this time for second degree burglary which carries a sentence of six months to fifteen years. It all started when an associate of mine informed me that he knew of a safe that contained a lot of money and that he needed an extra man to help him; well, at that time I was out of work, and money and was very desperate to make it on my own in order to relieve my sister of my burdens so she could properly care for her children. Needless to say I got busted and was back in prison. . . . On a charge such as mine (second degree burglary) a con gen-erally does from 15-18 months, with an 18 month-2 year tail (parole), but I did five years in with a five-year tail. I was assigned to the jute mill where gunny sacks were made. One had to be very care-ful when operating the machinery there, because it has claimed the loss of several cons' fingers, hands and arms, but the prison officials showed little or no concern to this at all, because if a con didn't put out the prescribed number of sacks (74) at the end of a work day, he would receive a reprimand the first time and a write-up every other time for which you receive disciplinary actions, resulting in being put into isolation. By me being new at this type of pro-duction, I was constantly behind, thus constantly in isolation, segregation, plus I was constantly harassed by the prison officials. The jute mill was burned to the ground one day by a new arrival who set fire to it. Cheers and sighs of relief could be heard through-out the whole prison when the mill went up in smoke that glorious day in 1951. . . .

The jute mill and prison officials were by no means my only problems in the pen. Survival in itself was a problem, for there were always personal clashes, race fights, even more race riots because racism was provoked by the prison officials and by me being a black man, my whole incarceration pe-riod was a perilous one. Whenever prisoners were being moved to chow, movie, or to their cells, they were always segregated. The only time they inte-grated was when they were out on the yard, well in sight of the gun towers, for it was a known fact that if a fight started, the officer in the gun tower would shoot the first black in sight whether he was involved in the fight or not. The gun tower officers were always comparing with each other and boasting about how many "Niggers" they had shot.

Animosity was imbedded deeply into me when I was granted parole for the second time in 1955, but what I didn't know at that time was the hell of all hells was yet to come. My second parole was almost identical to my first, I went jobless because whenever I found possible employment, my parole officer would contact the employer and tell him of my past. Well, no one wanted to hire a two-time loser. My sister's husband was struggling even harder than before because one of their children was ill and under medical attention and the bills were coming demanding payment; therefore they couldn't possibly afford to even begin to support me. I was now more desperate than ever. After only a few months out, I was busted again, this time for not only burglary, but robbery, too. I was found guilty on both counts plus the fact, three prior felony convictions were filed against me which enabled the judge to impose upon me 522b of the penal code. I was now labeled as a habitual criminal, which means that I would have to do twelve years before my first board appearance for parole consideration, but in 1965 I had one prior dropped which made it possible for me to make my first board appearance in nine years under that section (266C P.C.) which is the small habitual criminal act. At that time I had done only three months in the guiding center to be processed for my future residence.

When I left the pen I was in for what I never could envision in my worst dream. My new residence was hell's cesspool, the end of the world. "Stone" Prison made a Sunday School out of the pen, where I had been previously. Upon my arrival there I was

placed on fish row, which was on the fifth tier in
No. 4 Building. I was on fish row for a week, then
moved to No. 5 Building where I spent the next
seven years behind the screen which is Maximum
Security within the most maximum security prison
in this state.

In March, 1961, there was heavy tension throughout "Stone." It had always been a standard procedure to the prison officials to seat all Blacks in the
rear of the chow hall and after they had finished
eating, they were to remain seated until everyone
else had left the chow hall. It was so hot in there,
one would think he was in a boiler room. To rectify
this condition, a committee of Blacks (twenty-four
of us) went to see the Associate Warden to present
our predicament. Two of us were allowed to go into
the Associate Warden's office to discuss the situation. I was one of the two. The remaining 22 Blacks
were left standing outside. The Associate Warden
gave the two of us memos stating that the Blacks
could sit wherever they pleased while dining in the
chow hall. We spread the news throughout the prison, but we were in for a shock. At chow time only
about 200 of the entire population came to chow.
The total population was numbered at about 2500.
The Warden then called the State Prison Administration and stated that there were 24 Muslims who
had created a major uprising in "Stone" and that he
wanted them transferred immediately. We were
placed on a Greyhound bus under heavy guard and
taken to another Maximum Security Prison in this
state, and placed in the Wing which is the "Adjustment Center." Let me mention now that there was
only one Muslim among us. The state Attorney General ordered an investigation made of our allegations.

A black man and head of a local branch of the NAACP, and another black and a member of the Governor's Staff were assigned to the investigations. They took a statement from each of us in the A.C. Wing. They then investigated at the pen and came back to talk with us again. The blame was found to be on the prison officials at the pen.

I made my second board appearance on this commitment in 1966, and at this time I had eleven years in, but the board denied me parole and ordered that I be sent to a Minimum Security Camp Center. I needed a change and by this being a minimum security institution, I felt like an almost free man, but this feeling was soon to leave me. Not only was I denied parole again in 1967, I was rebellious against the working conditions and medical treatment one received while out at camp. In the winter it is cold and there is always snow on the ground, most of the time waist deep, but everyday they had us cons out there cutting not only trees, but ourselves too. In the summer, there were always forest fires to fight, resulting in cons being burnt and even losing their lives. There were also snake bites, but most of all there was always inadequate medical attention. I found there also a form of prison slavery: in exchange for risking his life and working harder than a free man working heavy construction, he was paid only fifty cents a day. My rebellious nature caused me to be returned back to the pen. I was again denied parole in 1968 and in 1969. I will mention here that the Parole Board officials consist of ex-prison officials, ex-police officers, ex-D.A.'s, ex-F.B.I. Agents, etc.

I began to wonder if I would ever receive parole, but in May 1970 a miracle, so to speak, was being performed in the form of a telegram from my sister to the Parole Board. It went something like this: "Almighty God, please let my brother come home to me, because as long as I have a home and piece of bread, he has a home and piece of bread." On July 13, 1970, I, Albert Johnson, A6158, walked out of the pen, yet I'm still not a free man. I have a lifetime tail (parole). My prison record is on file in the state capital. It has been there since 1946 under the same name and number: Albert Johnson A6158.

The Draft Resister
in Prison

David Miller

It's important when examining someone's opinions to know "where the person is coming from." Tales of prison life in these United States are no exception. I'm a young, white, middle-class college graduate who spent twenty-two months in federal prison for burning my draft card. The story of prison life that I relate centers around those facts. It would be the same for other draft-resister ex-convicts. The draft resister has a unique story to tell. There are many similarities with a lot of other prisoners, but there are important differences. Prison society is highly stratified. Draft resisters often walk a precarious line in and among various opposing hostile cliques and races in the prison setting. I want to offer a few words on what we share in common with fellow inmates, highlight some of the things separating us, then end with suggestions for a direction out of the maze all of us are in.

Inmates in American prisons are victims of a correctional process wholly lacking in socially redeeming value. The end products of our correctional systems are men and women humiliated, embittered, scarred, institutionalized, and often broken. Only infrequently do inmates come out of prison "better people" and it is always in spite of tremendous odds, at great personal cost, and never to the credit of the correctional process.

There isn't one prison administrator in the country who doesn't give at least lip service to the goals of rehabilitation and who doesn't have at least some semblance of a rehabilitative program for his or her charges. Prisons do, of course, vary in the amount and quality of their rehabilitative programs. But when the budgets for prisons throughout the country read 95% for custodial, administrative, maintenance, and other services and 5% or less for educational, training, and therapeutic services, outside observers can see what inmates know from painful experience. Security and control are the only real worries of prison administrators.

Adding the historical perspective, prisons and administrative methods for running them have changed over the years, but without altering the basic ingredients: punishment and humiliation. The penitentiary was introduced by reformist Quakers in Pennsylvania in the late 18th century. The penitent was expected to meditate in a cell over his or her sins and wrong-doings, and emerge from this bleak hole a changed person. This process was in opposition to being whipped or maimed. Along with the birth of the Auburn State Prison in New York in the 1820s, the penitentiary system begun in Pennsylvania was the harsh forerunner of modern penology. Solitary confinement and the infamous Auburn "silent system" reigned for nearly one hundred years. Inmates were infrequently, if ever, permitted to converse with one another, were made to do back-breaking work, and were dealt immediate physical discipline by the guards.

Today, inmates in American prisons are controlled in a much more sophisticated manner. Scores of archaic prisons still stand, but behavior manipulation tools like parole, good time, visiting, and recreational privileges elicit the docile conformity demanded by prison administrators. Guns and beatings are employed when necessary, but the day to day management of an inmate population is generally accomplished with pen and paper discipline, physical punishment remaining a real but somewhat more distant threat.

There is little useful work to be done in prison. Most work revolves around the needs of the institution. Inmates operate the laundry, the food service, the janitorial services, do most of the clerical work, and man construction and farm work details. "Correctional officers" supervise what prison officials call, with a straight face, "work therapy." There is scant motivation for the work and often ten people are set to work on a task suited for two.

Lack of normal heterosexual contacts and an exploitative homosexual milieu weigh heavily on the imprisoned. Young, susceptible inmates are preyed upon by small groups of aggressive homosexuals who exploit and degrade the so-called "passive" homosexuals in any institution. Prison administrators throw their hands up and say that prison homosexuality is difficult to control, that they do all they can to protect susceptible inmates from forcible assaults. The truth is that prison administrators profit from the perverted atmosphere they themselves maintain.

In every penitentiary there are what inmates call "jungle" dormitories. These dormitories are transient quarters that most inmates are put into shortly after arrival. Soon the newly-arrived inmate is transferred to better accommodations if he or she exhibits co-operative behavior. The jungle dormitories are the most crowded quarters in the penitentiary and are inhabited by the most unruly inmates. These inmates have been kept in the jungle dormitories because of their failure to "adjust." Prison officials use the jungle dormitories to threaten young inmates with sexual assault. The warden or associate warden will not say it directly, but when a young inmate is assigned to a jungle dormitory (it has been done with a number of draft resisters), it is saying, in effect, "Go ahead, see what you can do with this one." The desired result is to keep potential and actual protesters in line.

Prison officials do little to alleviate the tension building in prison sexuality when they actually have a mechanism available to help reduce it. The Prisoner Rehabilitation Act of 1965 was meant for the development of work release programs, but does provide for home visiting furloughs and other extensions of limits if the interests of society and rehabilitation are served. So far, the visiting furloughs have been granted only for funerals and sick bed visits. Apparently the interests of society and rehabilitation are not served by allowing inmates a regular opportunity to share a few moments with someone close to them.

Turning to the draft resister, the federal prison system holds approximately 200 draft resisters and anti-war activists in thirty-odd institutions across the country. Between coming and going, the number of currently imprisoned resisters has remained at the above level for the past years. The government could easily imprison thousands more young people who have refused to step forward. It could just as easily decline to imprison anyone for resisting the draft. The government's apparent policy is to imprison those resisters who are most notorious, who are most effective. Enough draft resisters must be imprisoned to make a visible deterrent. But locking up too many people (like raising the level to 2,000) would probably do more to build the anti-war movement than anything else.

The draft resisters are most heavily concentrated at federal prison camps in Allenwood, Pennsylvania and in Safford, Arizona. Allenwood is a minimum security farm camp sixteen miles from its parent institution, the penitentiary at Lewisburg. Allenwood has a population of 300-350 inmates, 100 of whom are Selective Service violators. Of that 100 there would normally be 75 Jehovah's Witnesses and 25 conscientious objectors. The term conscientious objector (CO) is prison jargon for selective service violators who are "political" and who do not fit into any other bag, i.e. Muslims, Jehovah's Witnesses, Amish, etc. Safford is a minimum security farm camp that has a contingent of 20-25 draft resisters. The rest of the imprisoned draft resisters are spread out in smaller numbers in institutions from Danbury, Connecticut to McNeil Island in the state of Washington.

[Note: the U.S. Disciplinary Barracks at Fort Leavenworth, Kansas and the U.S. Naval Brig at Portsmouth, New Hampshire are the two military prisons in the country. They house 30-40 military resisters. There are, of course, many hundreds in brigs and stockades around the world, but the more "political" of those are at the U.S.D.B. and Portsmouth.]

Draft resisters' sentences range from six months to five years. An increasingly popular sentence with judges is the Youth Corrections Act sentence which is an indeterminate sentence running from sixty days to six years. Most inmates dislike the "zip-six," as it's called, because the recipient is in a constant state of limbo. The rule of thumb for draft resisters is approximately two years, no matter what the sentence. If a resister had a sentence of two years, he would do it all (less good time) with virtually no chance of making parole. If a resister had five years or a zip-six, he would normally be granted parole after two years. However, "causing trouble" while imprisoned may quite well end in doing more time before finally making parole.

Draft resisters are nearly automatically awarded minimum security status and sent to farm camps after initial orientation in a penitentiary or correctional institute. Minimum security classification is no small advantage. The bearer is less supervised than his medium and maximum security counterparts, has opportunities (on paper at least) for programs outside the confines of the penitentiary, and in many cases resides in the more relaxed atmosphere of the farm camp (as opposed to the walled-in penitentiary). The only drawback of minimum security is the marshmallow feeling associated with being one's own keeper. Inmates at farm camps and those permitted on outside work details from the penitentiary can literally walk away from their captors. Being caught, though, means another two to five years added to your sentence; and the vast majority of such absconds are caught, more usually sooner than later.

The combination of a relatively short sentence with residence at a minimum security farm camp sometimes rests uneasily with draft resisters. Compared to inmates in the penitentiary, the draft resisters' lot looks to be a privilege and a cop-out. It is a privilege, relatively speaking, but I question whether it's a cop-out. Good sense alone would dictate that certain draft resisters stay at the farm camp since they would face real danger in the penitentiary from aggressive inmates whom the draft resisters lack the ability to handle properly. That is not the case for all resisters, but in the early stages of imprisonment many resisters find it difficult to adjust fast enough to a few of the harsher realities of prison life. Besides, every inmate owes it to himself to do the easiest time he can unless there is a solid resistance effort in the making.

Fellow inmates tend to view draft resisters in two rather desperate ways. On the one hand, the inmates are impressed with the good qualities the resisters exhibit. Draft resisters are well-educated, articulate, and thoughtful. We are idealists, perhaps extremely so, who have had the courage to stand up for our beliefs to the point of imprisonment. To men who, mostly through necessity, have seen their own higher inclinations go by the board as they steal to support themselves, the honesty and integrity of the draft resister is admirable. On the other hand, inmates see draft resisters as naive, arrogant, self-righteous kids who have little practical appreciation of some vital worldly principles even though the rhetoric might be there.

I would say that both strains, the admirable and

the naive, were present in myself and other draft resisters. While gaining the hard lessons prison dishes out and shedding the worst of our arrogance, the challenge that we faced was the retention and growth of what was truly admirable and humane in ourselves as those qualities were daily assaulted in prison life. There is no question that two years in prison changes people. The question is to what degree and in what direction.

Before prison I was a Catholic, a pacifist, and an anarchist. Today I'm none of those. My politics have undergone a rearrangement but I'll offer no categorization. Yet I think that I'm substantially the same person. Because I'm not an absolute pacifist as before, I am not then a killer. Neither do I attack the Church or those who believe. If I no longer find Catholicism or Christianity relevant to me, others do find it so for themselves. The commitment that continues to be mine is the desire to struggle with others for a better life, for an end to the war, for an end to oppression.

Prison is a crisis of faith and a crisis of action. The crisis of faith could be seen in the narrower sense of religious adherence. But I would not like to see it that way. The crisis of faith I'm interested in is not the acceptance or unacceptance of a religious doctrine. The crisis of faith I'm worried about lies in the confrontation between a young, strong, wholesome, trusting faith in self and others and the petty, jealous, cruel, callous, humiliating relationships we exist with in prison and most of all within ourselves. Prison life eats away faith in people and faith in self unless one strives to maintain it.

A crisis of faith necessarily leads to a crisis of action. Specifically, I'm afraid that many draft resisters, including the more political ones, are going to make their act of resistance a one-shot affair. I don't want to see anyone return to prison but I don't want to see people drop out of political work either. Our idealism and the brutality of prison must be reconciled in a way that enables us to continue. Injured perhaps, but not out.

Looking to the future, two serious problems confront draft resisters and others who are prepared to risk imprisonment in working for social change. Survival is first, resistance is second.

The government will continue to put protesters in prison. However, I'm not prepared to say that the federal government or any state government is going to imprison protesters in significantly larger numbers than is already in evidence. I fully believe, though, that the capability for doing so is there, that it would be done if it were politically expedient to do so, and that it would be avoided unless the authorities felt extremely threatened.

I don't believe that special camps are in the offing for draft resisters or any similar political groups. It's logical to assume that contingency plans exist but special camps would blow the cover off a political stance that the government is not about to relinquish at this time. The government insists that there are no political prisoners in the United States—only lawbreakers.

Survival means for me a strong effort at side-stepping imprisonment altogether. I will take political risks that could end in imprisonment. I think that is in the nature of political and social change. But staying out of prison is the first duty.

However, if a "fall" (term of imprisonment) comes my way, I'd spend the time in a manner most profitable for me by reading, talking, learning, in order to resume once again after release. I appreciate now, though, the road blocks involved in that path. The boredom, the lack of privacy, the lack of materials, the pressures of confinement, the escape mechanisms (TV, radio, sports), all conspire against you in prison. But it is terribly important for one's well-being, both in prison and afterwards, to understand these difficulties; and if they are not conquered completely, at least a bit of headway should be made through the waves. I found drifting a danger. I know that others did also and that in some cases it may take a year or more after release to put oneself together again.

Resistance may go hand in hand with survival but not always. The resistance waged by draft resisters, myself included, has generally been a pretty poor show. Characteristically it is spontaneous, individualistic, with ill-defined goals, and with little if any organized support on the inside or on the outside. True, the weapons that prison officials possess are awesome: arbitrary transfer, good time, parole, job transfer, a hands-off policy by the courts on "administrative" matters in prisons. But we must band together with inmates in prison and with ex-cons outside of prison to overcome the forces arrayed against us.

Inmates in New York City jails and in Attica State Prison were a jolting example of courage and daring. They put themselves on the line and are the shock troops of a new prison resistance movement. It's a turning point of major dimensions. But as powerful as their example may be, a movement can't be built around the tactic of taking over prisons and jails. It simply will not end advantageously for us.

Inmates and guards are killed and injured in the isolated take-overs. What is needed is a nation-wide, coordinated ex-con lobby backed by political pressure and demonstrations on the outside, and by other work within prisons.

Inmates and ex-cons should be organized on two levels. First: the anti-social elements in inmates' behavior has to be understood and dealt with. How did they get that way and what truly rehabilitative things can be done to patch up and change people who commit harmful acts? Offenders themselves must take a primary role in developing programs that actually help people, are viable alternatives to imprisonment, and safeguard innocent people.

Secondly, prisoners should understand their political position. While fighting the battle for prison reform, inmates and ex-cons must relate their struggle to the wider struggles for welfare reform, educational reform, an end to the war in Southeast Asia, and self-determination for oppressed peoples the world over. Prison reform is a distinct issue but it should not be a single issue.

An idea that came out of my experience is the prison house of hospitality. Wherever possible and wherever needed, houses of hospitality should be set up in towns adjacent to prisons to provide food and lodgings for the friends and relatives of inmates as they come through town to visit inmates at the prison. Many more relatives would be able to visit inmates if these services were present and those who do visit could visit more often. A network of prison houses of hospitality across the country could, through the medium of visitors, lead to a coordinated effort of resistance within our prisons.

The time is ripe for a prison resistance movement. Our job, the job of all concerned men and women, is to bring an emerging movement to fruition in the shortest amount of time, avoiding violence, and with the most benefit for all.

My Name Is George Wilson

George Wilson

My name is George Wilson. I am now in Southfield Residential Group Center, in Anchorage, Kentucky. I first started toward Southfields, or some other juvenile delinquent center, about the age of nine.

When I was about nine, I lived in a housing project in Louisville, Kentucky. I was then, and am now, the youngest in our family of ten, including my parents. I have four brothers and three sisters.

I'm not trying to make it look like it's not my fault, because it is, but the way I started getting involved in trouble was the example that my older brothers and father had set for me. Before my oldest brother joined the Army he and the next oldest to him were constantly out stealing and drinking.

Then after he joined the Army, the next oldest began stealing and drinking with the one under him. During all of this my father was constantly coming home drunk, and he and my mother began fighting, which then brought my older brothers into the fight. This happened at least once a week.

Then I and my other brother, next to the youngest, were stealing little things out of stores. Things like candy, bubble gum, balloons; anything that would get in our pockets. Although this wasn't a constant thing, just every once in awhile.

When we moved to First Street, my brother in the Army had been put in the pen, and received a dishonorable discharge from the Army. That is when the oldest after him joined the Army. And my oldest sister got married and moved away. This left seven at home. When we first moved to First Street, I was scared. It was a rough neighborhood, rougher than the projects. The kids were loud, wild, vandalistic. After the first few months of running, hiding, and getting beat up, I figured to join the crowd and be a real tough guy. So I started hanging with the rest of the gang and did mostly what they said to act big.

About this time Urban Renewal was starting to tear down and clean the whole neighborhood. This forced the people to move. I am about 11 now, and by now I'm right in the midst of the bad guys of First Street. And we were breaking into the empty houses and stripping the copper wiring and pipes out of every empty house within a 3 or 4 block square. We were also vandalizing the whole neighborhood. Knocking over garbage cans, busting every window that could be reached.

Then one day I and another guy were walking down the street and passed a house that was already broken into and about six kids had already started to tear the place up. So we went in, but there was a difference between this house and all the others we had gotten into. This house wasn't empty and the people hadn't finished moving. But now that we were in, it didn't make any difference.

So we grabbed two boxes of cut glass. There were pitchers, punch bowls, glasses, plates, and all together about a 20-piece dining room set. I took my box which had about eight pieces and went straight home with it. I don't know why I took it home. I guess because I had never stolen anything like it before. When I got it home my father told me to take it straight back to where I got it. I started to take it to a friend's house, but before I got there a man told me it was his house we got the stuff from, and that he woudn't call the police if we gave it all back to him. We both gave him all we took from the place, and he said there was more. So he called the police. The police picked me up at home about twenty minutes later. My father went down town with me. They didn't lock me up or nothing; just took my name, address, and finger prints, then let me go home. When I went to court, it was filed away.

I never got any type of punishment for it, although I was scared to death while it was going on. It didn't do any good. It just made me brag and act big because I got away with it.

Then finally we had to move. We moved to the east end of town to the corner of Clay and Ormsby. When we first moved there, I was surprised to see what a difference there was between the two neighborhoods. It was quiet, clean, and the only guys that did things like I did were in their teens. I had already started smoking and drinking before we got there, but not much of either. Now at about twelve, I was hanging with guys my age and not doing near as much as before. Although I was still stealing out of stores, after a few months of hanging with guys my age I was tired of it. Because I always had to do things by myself. So I started to hang with guys 15 and 16 years old.

Then I started cutting school with them. First

just lunch, then periods, and then whole days. While we were cutting, usually we were just running the streets waiting until time to go home. Then after a year or so I stopped hanging with the older guys because the guys my age were doing just as much as I was now.

At about 13 I started sniffing glue. I first did it to see what it was like and to act big. I sniffed almost every day I cut school, which was about three times a week, for about three months.

Until finally on March 2, my father's birthday, I got caught. At this time there was a big family fight and Mom and Dad were talking of a divorce. My father and I had a long talk that day and it hurt me very bad, and I never sniffed again.

When I reached the age of 14 I started cutting school much more and drinking more. I first started drinking by stealing my Dad's leftovers. Just enough to show off with. Then more and more until finally I was sending old "winos" to get it for me. At first I'd get a half pint of whiskey and go to the park and drink it. When I got drunk, I'd raise hell, tear up something, maybe get into a fight and sneak home.

At the most all I did for about a year was cut school, get drunk on week-ends and steal from stores.

When I was 15 I began not going to school at all. I would drink any time I got the chance; whether it was day or night, Tuesday or Saturday, it didn't make any difference anymore. I was staying out until 3 or 4 in the morning, and sometimes not coming home at all. I was my own boss. I stopped getting whipped and grounded because I wasn't so little.

When I was 15, on New Year's Eve I got locked up for drunk and disorderly conduct. I came out of a house where there was a party and started cussing the cops. They locked me and another guy up.

The other guy's mother got us out in about three hours. I didn't have to go to court or nothing. I then again bragged and told everybody about it, because I thought it was really something. After that, that's all I did—cut school, drink, steal small things like radios, fishing bait, cigarettes, and petty stuff. I was drinking more than ever now. I was drinking in bars, pool halls, on the streets; I was drinking with guys my age, and guys about 21–25, because if I drank with them I could drink in bars and pool halls and really act like the real big boys.

Although my father was an alcoholic, and came in drunk and willing to fight all the time, I was still very close to my father; closer than all my other brothers and sisters, I believe. Once when I was about 15½, we had some company over, and we were all playing cards. We were playing partners and my dad was sitting out. I and our next door neighbor were partners. My dad wasn't drunk; he wasn't even drinking, and he started raising hell at me for nothing.

I got up in a burst of anger and started out the door. When he stopped me, he told me to look at him when he was talking to me. So then I started out the door again, and when he stopped me the second time I hit him. That was the first and only time I have ever hit either of my parents. I was really hurt after that and I ran away the same day. That same night I went to the police station and asked an officer to lock me up and said I had run away. I could have stayed at some friend's house and bum for a week or so but I don't like to push myself on nobody. I had seen runaway guys and girls before, and after about a week or so nobody likes them, nobody wants to put up with them, and they are discarded as "poor runaway bums."

I stayed in Children's Center for about four days before I went home, and it was the most horrible place I had ever been to in my entire life. You had to fight or be a pushover. You had to fight to keep your own cigarettes, to eat, to sleep in peace, to sit down in a chair, to play cards; you had to fight or hide to stay alive in the joint. When I went to court they let me go home and that's it. After getting out of there I slowed down some, didn't do half as much for about a month.

Until one night, my brother and a friend woke me up about six in the morning. They said they had stolen four guns and wanted me to help get them into the house. So I got up, went down to the alley and got them.

They gave me a shotgun for helping them with the guns. The next day they went around trying to sell them. I had already sold mine on credit. And the next night the police picked me and my brother up at home. So then I went back to that "Hell Hole" called Children's Center. I stayed in for about five days before I went to court. I never thought I would get out of that place without either going crazy or getting killed.

When I went to court I was put on probation for six months. After getting out of the Center this time I was bitter and hated every cop, judge, probation officer or anything that had something to do with the law. I never kept my probation.

I never even tried to keep it. I was drinking more all the time. I had completely quit school, and was stealing anything I could get, except for the little stuff I had always gotten before. I ran in a pack of about nine other guys just like me. We stole anything, and when we got drunk we'd tear up anything, stores, bars, houses and sometimes jump people. We once broke in a house and took two TV's, radios, rings, watches, everything except for their furniture. And what we didn't get we tore up. Then a couple days later we all got drunk and broke into a bar. We took what we wanted and tore up the rest. It wasn't but just a few days after that we broke into a school. It was like a running fever. We broke into a pet shop 3 times, and two other bars all within about a month. One night I and another guy were riding with two girls and I was drunk as always.

While we were riding with the girls, the rest of my friends were breaking into a liquor store, that I didn't know nothing about.

The guys that had broken into the bar pulled up beside us, and I went with them.

When we got to the place they had already broken the window out and it was ready to walk right in and get what you wanted. So I and another guy went in, while the others waited outside in the car. While we were in we set off an alarm that we didn't know about. It was the kind that sounded at the police station but not at the bar.

When the cops came they got us and one of the guards outside; the others took off in the car. Once again I headed for that Center, that I hated with a passion.

I stayed in for about four days before going to court. When I went to court it was laid over until a later date. When I went back to court again, I had a lawyer and had it laid over for six weeks. This was to give me enough time to get a job and turn 16.

During this six weeks I stole nothing more. But I still drank as always. I looked for a job a few times but not with much real effort.

When I went to court for the final time I was sent to Southfields for a period of four to six months. I stayed in the Center for seven days before going to Southfields. It was seven days of pure hell. On May 24, 1971, Mr. Pollard, superintendent of Southfields, came and got me. With him was a guy from Southfields, who was my stick. We stopped and got another boy at his home to take him out with me. This made me feel much better, knowing that I wasn't the only new guy out there.

When we got to Southfields, it was a very pleasant change from the Center. There were no people trying to mess over me. Nobody tried to take my cigarettes, money, or nothing.

All the guys were friendly and willing to help in any way. All the people, including the staff, were very polite, and joked as if I knew them for years. There are no locked doors, bars or fences at Southfields. And anyone could walk off anytime they wanted to. When I first got here all I thought of for about two weeks was leaving. But before I could make up my mind, the guys of Southfields had made it up for me.

I was flat broke when I got there and the guys helped a lot. They gave me money to make phone calls, buy cokes, and gave me cigarettes without my even asking. We all work for the City Sanitation Department of Louisville, and get paid one dollar per hour.

If we worked 4 days a week we would get ten dollars, and eighteen would go in the bank for our release plans. When I first got here and decided not to go AWOL, I thought I'd pull time.

I kept thinking of the four to six months the judge said. But after listening in the group meetings, and to individuals outside the meetings I found time had nothing to do with getting released from Southfields. It all depends on you, whether you actually wanted to help or not. And the guys and staff can see whether or not you do. After being here I got a furlough. The trust they gave me was unbelievable. After being here just two days a three day furlough was given to me. The furloughs are given for you to get together with your parents and tell them your life story, all the wrongs they never knew about. And to discuss you and your future. But I never looked at it this way. I used my furloughs as a party time to make up for the future days I would be in Southfields.

All through my furlough I did nothing but drink and act big. When I returned I was jumped on by my group. They hollered and corrected me for my doing wrong. By this time I was tired of being a phoney and decided to "get real"; which was an expression used by many at Southfields. This meant, get serious, stop wasting time and get down to the real you, and try to change him. So I started, I began to talk up in my group sessions, and talk about my problems outside the group. When a guy first comes to Southfields, after being here a couple weeks he tells his life story the same as I have written here. And after this he gets his *problems,* which are titles for things that made you what you are, and made you do the things you did. Things such as a drinking problem, stealing, family, dope, sex, resenting authority. All these things are based on your story you tell and the guys in your group make them visual to you so you can accept and work on solving them with other guys. I have 15 problems and I would say drinking and acting big was the basis of all of them. After being here for about a month or so, I was no longer a new guy. I had assumed full responsibility like any other guy. After participating in the groups I found that guys really depended on me. And it made me feel good that somebody was asking me for help other than material goods. It make me feel good inside to be called upon by another guy to talk about a problem.

If the house stays straight and no major goofs are made we receive privileges, such as going to downtown Louisville to stay an entire day and return at seven that night, and dances with girls at other institutes, and furloughs.

Once on the 4th of July our group stayed here, and the other group went on a furlough. This was because our group's participation was poor and we had been acting up lately. So we stayed but our group improved very much also.

A few weeks later I asked for a furlough and was turned down. This made me mad and my bad attitude began to show. So the next week I asked again with the same bad attitude. Then I didn't know that that was what was keeping me from my furlough. So the next week I was turned down again, but I didn't get mad and pout. I accepted it as my fault and tried to work on my attitude. And the staff realizing this gave me my furlough because I wasn't such a sour loser.

I went on this furlough with a better attitude and at first really tried to make the best of it for my future benefit. So I told my story and stuck around the house for a while. But the same old guys I hung with, and the same surroundings won. I gave in and went back to my old self, except for the stealing. I never stole anything, but I drank and acted big as always. Although I did get rid of my stolen stuff I already had at home. I was told to do so by my group earlier. I threw away everything except for a gun and a camera. I was told to bring the gun back with me. And I couldn't see myself throwing away a good camera. The reason for bringing the gun back was because I couldn't get rid of it properly. So I turned it in here and no longer had it hanging over my head. After coming back I told about my furlough, but I didn't tell the truth. But my group leader found out the truth and gave me the chance to tell it to my whole group. So I told the truth and was climbed on vigorously by my group, not so much for screwing up, but for lying about it.

So as the days went past I was back into the feel of the house, and felt much better after seeing they still trusted me. So as I progressed at Southfields I began to see what a change I had made and how much more of a change I needed, and thought I was really doing good. Until one day I came in the house early without permission from any staff. There is a set rule that you don't come in the house until 3:30 because the city pays us up until that time. Well, earlier in the week I had smashed my finger in a car door. When we came home from work I went straight into the house to change the bandage. This was automatically a week in the pits for breaking Mr. Pollard's rule.

Now the pits are a restriction where you go out into a field and dig a pit, while the other guys are at work. While in the pits you make no contact with nobody. You're like a dummy. Nobody sees you and you see nobody. You take a water jug with you in the morning and if you forget it, it's just tough. You get one-half hour for lunch and go back out until the boys come in from work. Well, I made it through the pits, but thought I never would. While in the pits I thought of what I had done, and of the ignorance of it.

So as I prolonged my stay at Southfields, I found I didn't care for the things I used to want to do. I started to play basketball more and talk about my problems more than before. And as the newer guys came in I was being looked up to for help and I really tried to show them something. As the months went by I found another furlough facing me, and I wanted to show the group something with this furlough. So before we left I had made plans with the other guys to meet some of them on this furlough. So I did, and we had good fun without drinking or acting bad. But as it grew darker just riding and riding in a car got tiresome, and I went home. On this furlough my brother was at home from the Army on furlough. He had been at Southfields when he was younger. Later that night as things started to move, I started to walk the streets. And after getting with a couple bar friends, and shooting a couple games of pool, I went and got something to drink.

So I was up at a recreation joint when my friends from Southfields came in and took me home just inside of my curfew. So after talking with my brother and my friends from Southfields, I didn't drink anymore on my furlough. And I also didn't go around acting bad as I always did before. And after coming back to Southfields and talking with my group I could see where drinking did me no good at all—on my furloughs in the past, or what it will do for me in the future.

Now after getting back into the house with the rest of the boys I felt more comfortable than I did on the streets.

About a month after my furlough my Dad had a heart attack. This upset me very much. He went to Veterans Hospital and was put in intensive care. Mr. Pollard then let me go to the hospital and see him almost all day. I then asked for a furlough and was turned down because of my past with my furloughs. This didn't get to me much because I knew it was my fault for my past. But he did tell me he would make all necessary arrangements to see him.

So the next day I didn't wait for Mr. Pollard to make the arrangements. I called without permission and told my sister to come and get me. I went to the hospital and had my Mom call Mr. Pollard to ask for longer period of time to see my father. But he said no, and wanted me back in time for supper. So I came back and faced him with all my faults and he and I discussed the whole matter. And as I knew before I did it, I was completely at fault. So I was sent back into the pits for an indefinite period of time. This means until I could show that I was ready to come out. Although I was sent to the pits he still let me go see my father several times after that. He and the rest of the staff were very concerned about the whole matter. Well, he brought me out of the pits after three days and I was very glad to hear it. The pits are the hardest restriction at Southfields. My father soon came out of the hospital and was feeling much better. And I felt much better to see that the staff were happy to see it. They actually cared about my father. Now I figured there would be some concern, but it surprised me to see how it relieved them.

I am now an "old boy" of Southfields. This means I am one of the top seven guys who are responsible for the whole house's actions. We are to set an example for the newer guys, and control the house. Being an "old boy" is hard for me, but I think with enough help from the other boys I can make it. After being here for almost 5½ months I have accomplished a lot. I have not only seen my wrongs and faced them, but I have overcome my bad habits. I have also learned to stop and think before I do something, and listen to every man's opinion and give other people just as much a chance as you would want. And to stop and think would it be worth the consequences after doing it. And now after almost 5½ months, I sit here in Mr. Pollard's office and look at the walls covered with pictures of other Southfields guys. I wonder what problems they had, and how difficult they must have been.

I hope for the day when I can have my picture up there with the rest of the "Southfields Graduates."

Church and State in Prison

Patricia Halloran

My juvenile hall was warm and friendly—better than home sometimes—so it was never too frightening (after the first time) for me to go there. All of my friends were there, and I got along well with the counselors. I even looked forward to going there at times.

This time, though, I was leaving to go to a strange and foreign place. The judge had put me into the custody of the CHURCH. I was on my way to a girl's institution run by the nuns. I wasn't a "good" Catholic, although I had been forced into being baptized by my parents when I was twelve. I was thirteen now, and a ward of the State and the Church.

My life that led me into this multi-warded state, was a juvenile life of juvenile crime . . . run-away and skipped school. I didn't come from a split-home (divorced or separated parents), or from the ghetto, but from a house that emotionally starved and neglected me. As long as there was food on the table three times a day, and clothes on your back, you were supposed to be "just fine." I perhaps wanted more, and at that age had trouble verbalizing my needs, yet they were real. My parents were regretful, but willing to give me up to the State and Church, since they felt "they just couldn't handle me."

After the first time of running away and being placed in "juvie," my probation officer recommended that I be put in a foster home. I was, and did go . . . but I began to like it there, and had a lot of guilt feelings that I shouldn't like it, because I wasn't with my parents. Then after an episode with my foster father—he came home late one night, and got into bed with me—I ran away. I could not relate what had happened to my probation officer (I felt like I had caused the whole thing) so the only alternative (?) was to place me into an institution.

When I got back from court, and told my friends where I was going, there were a lot of stories that were told to me, about what they do to you there . . . scared me to death, I even contemplated suicide. But, after all the horror stories (my friends who had never even been there decided to tell me that they were all lies) I began to look forward to going . . . something different, new faces to meet and a challenge for me to get along with people.

The car ride over to the institution didn't cheer me up though. I was transported like a common "criminal," police car and all. I tried to pretend nobody could see me in the back seat. The transportation officers (one man, one woman) didn't talk to me except to tell me when to get in and when to get out. They were busy discussing how tired they were of getting all of the juvenile cases, and wanted more excitement in their work. (Maybe I should have tried to escape, but I was too worried about where I was going to think of how to escape from a police car that has no door-handles in the back seat.)

I can remember straining my eyes looking all

over the area as we were driving up, trying to see what it looked like, and then seeing this huge big brownish-yellow stone (cement) building, and it looked like what I thought San Quentin looked like. It was big, and it was cold looking . . . criss-cross bars on the windows, strings of barb-wire between buildings, and about four stories high. You couldn't see inside the walls, and from where I was looking it looked like you couldn't even see out, much less get out. (Already I was looking for places to split from.)

We pulled right up in front of these huge double doors, and as my door was opened by the police, the door to the building opened up . . . it just seemed to swing open by itself, as though it knew I was there, and coming in. The nun who opened it was behind the door, and shut it when we cleared the entrance. It sure did remind me of a recent horror-movie with the door creaking open, and once you were inside, "they" had you at their mercy.

After a little paper work, I was deserted by the two police officers, who were still talking about their dull job. I was relieved of my suitcase, and asked to follow a huge figure in flowing white robes, with black head gear. I couldn't see her face or her shoes . . just a creepy figure going down a long corridor. Smells of Pine-Sol disinfectant, wax and cold marble came at me from the floor to ceiling. Something like a hospital . . . only instead of alcohol or ether you get wax and Pine-Sol. There were no people in the hallway, or voices either. I thought for awhile that everybody was gone, but I soon found out it's always like that. People are there, you just can't see them, or hear them.

I was taken to the "infirmary." Even though I

wasn't sick, that's where they take all of the new people . . . sort of an isolation for medical and psychological reasons. Medical, to keep you isolated in case you have a disease, psychological, so that you are so lonely and frightened you can be led around real easy by a bunch of nuns. The infirmary had six beds in it, and hardly anything else . . . no TV, or radio or books. You just had beds with white sheets and bedspreads on them to keep you company. The questions I asked the nun who took me there were, "Is this where I live?" "Are there any other new girls here?" "When do I eat?" "How long do I have to stay here?". . . all these questions were left unanswered except for "Someone will come and tell you."

She left, and I heard her turn the key in the door from the outside. I went over and checked it out anyway—maybe she was fooling. She wasn't. I was in there and had time on my hands.

I lay on the bed, and tried to convince myself that I wasn't afraid of anything, and that I didn' care that I was there, and that they couldn't do any thing to me anyway. . . . I soon found myself crying because everything I told myself, I told myself back that I was afraid and that there was a lot they could do to me because look at the way they had treated me already. Wasn't I a human being, and I wasn't a "bad" girl, and that I'd never hurt anybody in my whole life. Boy, I was sure getting scared now. didn't want to stay here at all . . . they could have and I wanted out. I had been there a total of thirt minutes. Thirty years could have passed for all knew: I was going to have to stay there and di there. See, once the judge turns you over to the nun it's up to the nuns when you get out. Not the judge

And the way we were starting out our relationship, the Church and me, it didn't look good.

The mind plays tricks on you when you are lonely and scared, so I was talking out loud to myself trying to build up my confidence, when the door opened up and a different nun, this one in all black, came tripping into the room, and laid a tray with food on the table, and then waltzed out the door again. I was embarrassed because she had caught me talking to myself, and a little slow in blurting out my question of when do I get out, because my words bounced off the locked closed door. It was getting dark now, and I was hungry, so I ate the food and didn't bother turning on the lights, because I didn't know where the switch was (it was outside I found out later) so I was totally alone (repenting of my sins by this time) in the dark.

I fell asleep with my clothes on, and when I woke up, it was morning and I still had the tray in the room from dinner, so I knew no one had come in during the night. I could have been dead for all they cared, I thought. That made me mad (and scared) so I started yelling for help. Pretty soon, the key in the lock turned, and there were two nuns this time . . . so I figured they had heard me, and were coming to get me out. Right away I started smiling and saying hello, and how are you and trying to be friendly-like. One told me to wash up and follow her. I wondered where we were going. I soon found out. To mass. I had to sit next to the nun, and in the back to ourselves. The other girls were up front, and they turned around a lot checking me out. My face was sore from all the smiling I did during that hour of praying. I was praying that I could talk to someone and get the hell out of that infirmary. My prayers

weren't answered, or heard, for after mass, before
the rest of the girls went out, the nun signalled for
me to follow her. Back to the infirmary I went. How
long did I have to stay there? The nun told me until
the doctor had seen me. When was that? Soon, was
the answer. Not why, or who, but just soon.

Another tray was delivered and I ate that too . . .
don't know what it was, didn't much care . . . eating
alone isn't too much fun.

The doctor was an old man, fat and bald, and
not too much friendlier than any of the nuns I had
met. He gave me a physical and asked me how many
kids I had and if I ever had gonorrhea. I thought he
was kidding. I was only thirteen. Didn't matter to
him, though.

It was late in the afternoon of the second day I
was there before anyone came in and finally talked
to me. I was told all of the rules, even given a five
page book on do's and don'ts of the institution. The
nun told me that if I minded my own business, and
didn't get involved with the wrong crowd, I wouldn't
have too bad a time there. She didn't smile at me
once, and I felt like this was her only job . . . telling all
the new girls what to do and what not to do. She
really didn't care if you got along or not, she just
had her job to do, and God loved her for it. (I was
really beginning to hate them all.)

Some of the rules that really hit me were the
ones on talking. You couldn't talk in line, in the
dining room, in school, in church, or during study
period in the cottage. I wondered if you could talk
at all. Also, you were given 10 points a week, (if
you were good) and after you had 150 points, you
could go out of the institution with your family or
guardian for one hour, once a month. One-hundred

fifty points I added up to over three months . . . shit, that was a long time without going out of these walls, I thought.

My move from the infirmary to the cottage was without incident. I was going to the cottage after dinner and during study period so no one talked to me when the nun brought me over. After I had put my few things in the dresser assigned to me next to my bed, I went downstairs to see what was going on. I sat down in a chair next to a brown sister, and started asking her questions. She didn't answer me, and gave a funny (but sympathetic) look, and a nun swooped down and told me that talking wasn't allowed, and hadn't I been informed of the rules? When I answered yes, she took a little black book out of her tent of cloth, and asked me my name, and put a check next to my name. I had just lost 10 points! A whole week's worth of points. What a good start, I thought, I am a chronic talker, and this wasn't going to get me very far out the gate at all!

The beds were upstairs, twelve beds to a dorm, two dorms all together, with the nun's room connecting the two. There were three beds to a row, with dressers separating the beds. All the same color, and all very army looking. The smell of Pine-Sol and wax was here too, right in your own bedroom. The girls came up to get ready for bed now, and a few stopped by to meet me. They were nice, but had sort of an attitude that they had been there for awhile, and that I should know where I stood. The word had gotten out that I had gotten points off already, which gave me a little status with them from the start. I told them the nuns could take their points and shove them. I acted like I couldn't care less about anything. You have to act that way in the beginning, so no one thinks you're a snitch or fink. The tougher you act the better it is for you. But not too tough, or the girls will think you are a big shot, and test you out. I didn't want to fight (especially since I had never fought with anyone besides my sister, and wasn't too hot on getting beat up).

The days turned into a routine, up at 5:30, with the nun standing in the doorway holding her prayer book, but keeping one eye on us. Then we line up and march to church. After mass, we march to the dining room for breakfast. All this in silence. Then we go back to the cottage and get our books for school. Lunch is the only break we have, and then back to school till four. We get to go out in the yard and play, or just sit around and talk, since there really isn't too much playing equipment to play with. The play yard is made out of asphalt and is in the center of four buildings so that we were completely walled in. No gun-towers on the walls, but we were just as secured. Dinner was at 5:30, and at 6:30 we were marched back to our cottages and study period began. At 8:00 we could turn on the T.V. if the program was approved by the cottage house mother (nun), and at 9:00 we went to bed. If you wanted to shower, you had to do that between 8:00 and 9:00.

This was the schedule Monday through Friday and Saturdays were cleaning and studying and Sundays were just as dull. Sometimes there was a break in the daily routines, like the time one of the nuns that had been living on the nun's side for twenty years in solitude, praying for the world's salvation died. I, nor anyone I knew had ever seen or heard of this nun, but after dinner one night, we all were lined up to go sprinkle "holy" water over her as she lay in her casket. I had never seen anyone dead before, and it frightened me, I didn't want to go in the room, but we were all told we "had" to. This only happened once while I was there, but it was enough for a lifetime since I can still see how yellow and waxish she looked, and dead.

By the end of the first month, I was 350 points in the hole, which meant I had to make up the points and it would probably take me over a year before I was going to be eligible for an outing outside. Visiting was one Sunday a month, one to four in the afternoon.

After I had been there for several months, I asked how long I was going to have to stay there, and the head nun told me until I graduated from high school. I was in my first year. I didn't want to be there even for another month, so the next afternoon, I ran away. I climbed up on the ramp leading to the main building and hung from the bottom of the third story window, and jumped (or just let go). When I hit the ground, the breath was knocked out of me, and I sprained my ankle, but I was up and running before I could catch my breath.

It didn't take me long to get caught. . . . I think I was turned in by my parents the same day that I split. I went home, since I didn't really have any place else to go.

From then on, it was one institution after another until I was twenty-one years old. I got charged with escape when I split from the convent, and that became a bigger offense than my previous run-away.

One thing about all of the rest of the institutions, is that basically they were the same . . . bad. But, as I can tell from the way the words on the past few pages poured out of me, the first one left its mark. I don't know what the answers are, but I do know that we better start looking to ourselves and in the communities rather than giving up people to "institutions" run by people who don't care or even understand the problem. We have created bureaucratic monsters called institutions. We have to understand them to deal with them.

Sure, I might have survived the whole trip, but was it really necessary? And, there are many people who don't live through it . . . they become nuns, or criminals. And either life is not with the community.

Prison

James Douglass

In my trial I am called to bear witness to the truth with my life. Bearing witness to the truth means walking the way of truth: that way in America may lead to prison. For the way of truth is the way of liberation—the liberation of all humanity—and thus the way to prison in the midst of a warfare state and economic empire whose prosperity is built on the enslavement of an unseen world. The risk of prison in America is the condition of my deepest freedom because without that risk of truthful living I am already in a prison of my own making, a prison of fear and of self.

What is there to fear, man?

I fear what they can do to me. It is a fear which runs from my seeing it directly, but a fear which I feel identifying itself with all that I have now and would lose—if my fear should be realized, and they should take it all away.

Take what away?

Everything I have.

Like what, for example?

Well, if you want an inventory: job, home, friends, reputation, a way of life which adds up to a secure existence for my family and myself. I fear

much more for my wife and family than I do for myself. I have no right to neglect their needs because
of my own feelings of conscience. My first duty is to
my wife and family.

Your wife is as capable as you are of resistance.
Women and men resist together in Indochina. It is
in America that men feel such unique obligations
toward women: pots and pans for the American
women, napalm for the Vietnamese. Let your family
—wife, husband, and children together—be a family
of resistance. Grant them all the dignity of entering
the real world, where most families suffer while yours
prospers.

And what if they refuse?

Then listen, man:

I have come to set a man against his father, a daughter against her mother, a daughter-in-law against her
mother-in-law. A man's enemies will be those of his
own household. Anyone who prefers father or mother to me is not worthy of me. Anyone who prefers
son or daughter to me is not worthy of me. Anyone
who does not take his cross and follow in my foot-
steps is not worthy of me. Anyone who finds his life
will lose it; anyone who loses his life for my sake
will find it.

That's going too far.

Just far enough to speak to your condition.

Jesus Christ, you make a very complex matter
sound simple. I want to speak to a theologian instead. Or even a bishop.

You know the theologians and bishops are all
asleep at this hour. It is simple. Listen again: "Happy
are those who are persecuted in the cause of right:
theirs is the kingdom of heaven. Happy are you

when people abuse you and persecute you and speak
all kinds of calumny against you on my account."

Jesus, what a way to live.

The way—entered by a narrow gate.

I've heard all that.

Then believe it.

Gandhi believed and translated it into the context
of his own imperialist state:

For me solitary confinement in a prison cell without
any breach on my part of the code of Non-cooperation
or private or public morals will be freedom. For me
the whole of India is a prison even as the master's
house is to his slave. A slave to be free must con-
tinuously rise against his slavery and be locked up in
his master's cell for his rebellion. The cell door is
the door to freedom.

The cell door is the door to freedom because
once I am prepared to walk through that door I have
nothing to fear. They—whoever "they" may be, perhaps even human beings like myself—can instill no
deep fear in me if I am willing to accept the sub-
stance of their threat and travel the Way with whatever consequences it may bring. The cell door is the
door to freedom if I can acknowledge its threat as
the promise of the kingdom.

Nevertheless I am conscious that once I have
passed into that cell my freedom can be no Gospel
ideal or revolutionary slogan but can only take the
form of an experience realized within me, or if not
realized, then acknowledged as an illusion. I know,
from the few weeks I have already spent in prison
for acts of civil disobedience, that a profound sense
of freedom behind bars is possible, precisely as
Gandhi describes it, but that the experience is likely

to diminish as the time behind bars lengthens. In contemplating prison consequences which may be measured not so much in days and weeks as in months and years, I must confront the reality of prison not as an interlude in a white middle-class existence but as a stage of the Way re-defining the nature of my life. Prison is then of such duration and intensity that from within the experience I am forced to come to terms with prison as the context of my very life. How free can the choice of prison (through a deliberate act of civil disobedience or a chosen way of life which invites prosecution by the State) remain for me when the severity and duration of my sentence seem to absorb my very life, and instead of feeling myself passing through the role of prisoner I *become* the State's prisoner? What will my sense of freedom be at that point where my principal identity in terms of the institutions of my society is no longer citizen but prisoner?

The question has no answer because no person can know in advance how much he or she can endure for the sake of truth and still come up singing freedom. I cannot know if my belief is rooted deeply enough to sustain me through the worst. The posing of the question is no more than a prayer—a confession of my ultimate powerlessness. But the prayer can be extended into a meditation, and by exploring the resources to sustain my experience of freedom behind the cell door I can know better how solitary my confinement will be.

I remember the valley I was born into, a valley which introduced me to the Way. The Way was present in the valley as the sun and shadow which filled the valley without even being exhausted by it. Sun and shadow climbed down and up the rock shale

and cliffs, over and under the pine trees, sun and
shadow moving across the mountain slopes at the
edge of the sky, and as night fell, sun fading out
overhead as bright stripes in the blue and shadow
looming into darkness below.

The Way was in this silent light and change of
the valley which filled my being, poured through it,
saying nothing but passing my life through day and
night, light and dark changes, like the valley's river
rippling over a rainbow of rocks which gleamed and
disappeared in the flow of light and shadow. The
Way was in the silence of the valley, which if one
listened to distinguish, was wind brushing trees, river
flowing, a car's tires on the highway, and a dog
barking down there. So a thinking kind of listening
would note that the valley had many sounds in it,
which could be accounted for in different ways, but
the Way was that flow of life through the Valley
which remained silent as it entered my being.

The Way of sun and shadow reached in and
touched me at the center, and when I looked closely
was all of the valley withdrawing into darkness
again. I knew the Way as giving itself in the deepest
silence. No one ever referred to it. The name "Way"
came later as I realized I was walking in it, though
I no longer lived in the valley.

I learned to walk in the Way by letting go of the
thinking kind of listening, as one did in the valley,
and letting silence enter. Another name for the Way
was "Guiding Touch." It was no more than that, a
touch at the center, and again if I tried to watch too
closely it dissolved and there was only myself watching. But its guidance was real and had to be followed: It meant while walking along a way I had
assumed (or been told) was right, that I would stop

suddenly one morning with people passing on eithe
side, listen, turn slowly, and with utter certitud
walk in the opposite direction. If anyone was nea
enough to notice, the only explanation to an astor
ished look or question was simply that I'd lost th
Way and it lay not there but here.

Finding the Way was not always that simple
and a struggle with it gave me my first experienc
of prison. I recall a certain point in my life whe
I began to define my work by the talents of a frier
working alongside me. My friend's talents were fe
greater than my own and seemed required by th
nature of the work itself. At first I struggled to ove
come my limitations by increasing the pace and reac
of my work, trying to jump across great gaps in m
abilities and understanding. But my sense of my lim
tations deepened and what little understanding I ha
become confused. The Way was lost, and my situe
tion became inexplicable. It made no sense to hav
walked this far with certitude, then to discover tha
my limitations blocked any further progress. Becaus
I *had* to go forward yet had no possible way to c
it. I thrashed as one drowning in deep water ar
went under, to exist as dead matter for what seeme
a very long time. The living, caring universe becan
a gray room in which I sat listlessly or got up to pac
occasionally. Nothing and no one could change th
fact that I was inwardly dead. Time moved nowher
I was in prison, locked into myself.

Yet one day while pacing I glanced up and di
covered that the Way had begun to re-open befo
me. It had been impossible to see it in terms of n
own ambitions, which had finally collapsed so cor
pletely that when I looked up, the Way had r
emerged. By defining the end myself I had destroye

e Way, which led elsewhere. I had forgotten the alley, which realized its life through silence. When e valley's silence sang its way in once more, I felt would never be so arrogant as to lose it again by elf-definition, but I did several times and experienced a still harsher imprisonment.

The Way always moved out beyond calculation nd thus demanded faith to walk in it. It made no ense to anyone who wanted to secure his future. It emanded that one give up more and more to continue on it. It opened into a sky-clearing light only ter a long walking in darkness. The Way then became one in my understanding with the Way of Jesus f Nazareth whose life spoke in the same silence of un and shadow as the valley did, and whose death-reaking symbols of cross and open tomb declared at the Way was impossibly demanding and incredly life-giving. Jesus said with his life, death, and surrection that the Way, when followed in a hostile orld, meant love and faith to the point of revolu-on. Jesus' life said redeem the times—not with your wn strength, for you have none and will be destroyed if you rely on it—but redeem the times by ining with others in a community of faith and re-stance to death because the Way of Resurrection emands it. My suffering people, the human family, emands it. Truth and love demand it. Your very ing demands it. And if you meet the demand, the 'ay of the valley will sing its deepest silence, its arpest beauty, into your being in the life-giving rm of a cross.

Jesus' Way led to his imprisonment, and with nprisonment, execution, the foreseen conclusion of way of truth which he declared would make people ee. How can my choice of prison, through a delib-

erate life of resistance bearing that consequence, b
understood as a liberating stage of the Way?

Prison is the primary weapon in the State'
domestic war. That war begins with the studied ma
nipulation of public opinion against "crime in th
streets" to support the sharp build-up of tactical po
lice squads to control insurgency in ghetto areas an
counter-culture communities. Riot-control and con
spiracy laws are passed as a formal declaration o
war against internal enemies: black people wh
won't wait and young people who won't conform
Once the law-makers have declared war, the polic
and the courts wage it with dedication. The purpos
of the penal system in that war is to force the State'
enemies to their knees. What the American bombin
plane is to Indochinese peasants, the threat and us
of the penal system is at home to poor, mostly black
Americans: a technique to force subject peoples t
remain in colonial roles for an imperialist powei
Jacques Ellul's analysis of technique in the moder
state, in which means overwhelm ends and any pos
sible human dimension in the name of rational eff
ciency, has special application to the penal system
Our prisons are techniques for America's violer
control of her rebellious poor, and in recent day:
increasing numbers of young political resisters. T
claim any further purpose for these institutions is,
believe, to dignify them beyond reality. From th
experience I have had both within them as a prisone
and visiting others in them, I believe that their clea
purpose is raw power in the service of a ruling clas

Today we are all creatures of technique, and
is commonly felt by those in opposition to the State
power that to submit to that power to the extent c
becoming a prisoner (through resistance) is to b

come ineffective in the struggle for change. The way
to meet the State's technique, it is argued, is by more
effective technique, the way to meet power—greater
power. It is obvious that going to prison makes no
sense in the struggle for power.

But this kind of opposition to the State's power
and technique, while opposed to it in politics (Left
versus Right, Cleaver versus Reagan), is in fundamental agreement with its spirit, the spirit of technique. Effectiveness is the determining gauge of value,
and it is assumed that everyone knows in general
what being effective is and wants to be a part of it—
for the sake of the solution. Determine the one best
means for each step to power, then make it work.
Thus one proceeds through the various grades of
political, psychological, and physical force in order
to reach a liberating end which becomes less and less
visible in the process.

The way of effectiveness runs counter to liberation. To be effective is to be determined in action by
a calculated end and means. Thus the philosophy of
calculated action, which in the Western World means
a pragmatism verging on violence, is our determining
factor in making effective decisions. The philosophy
of calculation bears with it an assumed relation between the person and his goal of action which is in
reality a profound bondage, as Hinduism has taught.
In struggling to find and use the one best means or
technique, I am so binding myself to a mentally pre-
determined end that my desire for success, for the
fruits of action, is dragging me farther and farther
down into myself. My rationally chosen technique—
whether it be the bombing of North Vietnam or the
bombing of an ROTC building—compels me into an
attitude of self-determined ends which becomes less

and less capable of acknowledging the resistance o
reality, which will not respond to my techniques b
granting me my ends. As frustration mounts, th
philosophy of technique will always argue for mor
forceful means—"escalation"—whose recurring lac
of results (toward a dimly remembered value) wi
deepen my bondage to self and ultimate futility.

Thus the end effect of effectiveness for alread
established power, in the Pentagon and State Depart
ment, is an almost total withdrawal from the rea
world into a technological game room, a computer
ized self, whose automated thunder won't work o
Vietnamese peasants. But although impotent in thei
power, the great danger of policy-makers is that thei
volcanic frustrations will pitch them into the ultimat
act of effectiveness, global self-destruction: destroy
ing the world to save it.

The same suicidal effect of technique on self i
seen in the revolutionary whose unsuccessful strat
egies for power are marked by a deepening rhetorica
insistence that power be seized, by any means neces
sary, the means in each case failing more obviousl
to achieve his objective until his alienation from
reality is complete.

Technique is effective in binding the self to itse
and away from an engagement with reality. As
means of liberation, the philosophy of technique i:
in a literal sense, self-defeating. It is a means c
solitary confinement more destructive of a person
freedom than any imprisonment the State can in
pose.

The Way, however, is not effective. It is free
Jesus lived and died for no self-determined end b
to fulfill the Father's will at the center of his being
Gandhi following the teaching of the *Bhagavad-Gi*

continually renounced the fruits of his actions, in contrast to his political allies, and remained free of the struggles for power which divided and almost destroyed independent India. The Way is free because it is a way not of technique and self but of openness and Being. The Way of Jesus and Gandhi is the way of liberation because, in being responsive to the suffering and injustice of the human family, it is faithful in every stage of its response to that creative truth of Being which loses its self for the life of all. Being is one. Those who live in its Way are radically free through the gift of themselves in Being's fundamental act of self-emptying love. The Way re-creates in the soul of those who walk it, through the gift of themselves, the union of all creation in the fullness of God. Those who live in the Way are the givers and receivers of freedom because they realize the self-denying, self-fulfilling truth that the purpose of freedom is to create it for others.

Prison as the accepted price of resisting mass murder for the sake of reunion is a liberating stage of the Way because it repudiates in an act of Being the self-confinement of technique which is the most profound form of our common bondage, rulers and resisters alike. The choice of prison as a stage of the Way liberates one from the same bondage of technique and force which is the underlying principle of prison's threat to the self. If that choice of Being by the resister is made deeply and radically enough, the self-confining effect of prison will have been nullified from the beginning by the self-liberating rejection of effectiveness.

The choice of prison through resistance is technically ineffective and spiritually explosive: Gandhi, Bonhoeffer, the Berrigans, and thousands of young

American war-resisters who by living out their truth
behind bars are radically altering lives—their own
and others—all speak to the point. If my choice of
prison through resistance is to be sustained in me as
it has been in others, I must renounce all ends from
the beginning (What end can be served by my silence
behind bars?) and give myself fully to the silence
of a way which offers no guarantees for truth and
love. The valley of sun and shadow is a long way
from prison but I believe that prison, like death or
a cross, can in faith open a way into a valley of
silence where life flows without ceasing.

One Meaning of Prison in America

Chuck Barrett

I guess the first thing to do is to make this article legitimate by telling you that I have pulled some time some few times in my life. But don't get me wrong; it hasn't been a long time, not years, not even months mostly. It hasn't been in big state pens but in little county jails. Deep Southern (Baptist) County jails. Mostly my offenses have been genuine attempts (unsuccessful attempts) to disrupt the lawful and orderly processes by which the Power of Death manages to manage this world. The only trouble was, that for all my marching around Jericho (and heel-cooling in Ninevah), I was unwittingly helping to usher in the new Civil Rights Bureaucracy and Equality Under (the iron heel of) the Law. With it came the New Criminal Justice, the New Penology, the rule of Technique and the management of human behavior by the State. I am sorry. And that is the point of my article.

For now I am working in a maximum security adult felon prison in our Southland and I feel right at home. I am here to contend against those same Powers I previously helped to enthrone in the name of liberalism, the new theology, and the "let's-do-something" type of church relevance. But the point is that I *feel* right at home. That has something generally to do with the fact that I have been to school and college in America, and specifically to do with the fact that I have been to three seminaries in America. Because the realities of both are the same. That is why the poor bedeviled students are burning them down. That is also why, when they do try it, they will regret it because they will end up in prison and they too will feel right at home. Horribly so. The chances are that they will go to a prison that is, to one degree or other, coming under the sway of the new technological "let's re-structure, let's rehabilitate, let's prosocialate" psycho-social blasphemies of progressive penology. Under the blinding sear of the operating room lights of white-coated, tie-suited hosts of Mackflecknoes psychologiste, sociologiste, voc. specialiste, ed. specialiste, o.j. technologiste, etc., etc. . . .

When a child of God trembles and shakes into the place where I work, he is analyzed (in absentia) for some several weeks and then he is "classified" and given his "initial prescription" (I kid you not) of therapies, trainings, schools and "self help" groups. *If he does not follow this prescription designed in his absence he will not be recommended for parole. FOR FREEDOM!*

Since the program is not relevant at all to him, since it is nearly forced on him, he hates it. But, nearly to a man, he follows it. And that's where it gets interesting. It becomes a deadly serious game of wits. He hustles the PROGRAM, the PROGRAM attempts to remake him. It is a war. IT IS THE TYPE OF WAR THAT WILL CHARACTERIZE THE LIFE OF EVERY PUBLIC OR PRIVATE

SCHOOL CHILD, EVERY WORKER, EVERY TAXPAYER, EVERY CONSUMER, EVERY TEACHER, EVERY PRISONER, AND, God help and deliver us, EVERY CHURCHGOER in America's now-flowering future.

Prison is the proving ground for new human behavior control and modification systems. I am told they started the new penology at this prison around 1969. In 1970 I began to read about the new educational experiments in New York City and Durham, North Carolina that center on testing six year old children for future criminal, delinquent, and antisocial tendencies. The testing is followed up by placing the children (per results) in "different" school patterns—*one of which is the "correctional reform pattern."*

I do not hate the people who operate and design these programs. They are victims themselves. My fight is not against God-created human beings. They and I will be judged together by a far greater Righteousness and a far greater Mercy.

I was told the following story by a lawyer in a courthouse hallway. I give it to you as a parable. "A jury was trying a rape case and had been deliberating for hours over the verdict of an apparently open-and-shut case—clear-guilt—when the clerk came out of the jury room and announced in a whisper to the judge that the jury was hung by one member who refused to vote her verdict. The judge called the juror into his chambers. In came an old black woman, thin and bent and neatly dressed. The judge asked her why she couldn't reach a decision in such a simple case. The old woman looked at him out of the depth of her years and quoted him some Scripture out of Matthew. Then she said it was against her religion to render a verdict on another human. The judge fumed, shouted, reminded her of her oath, threatened her with contempt, and when the woman, obviously uneducated, refused to change her stand, he broke down and had her ushered from the courtroom and her name stricken from the rosters of eligible jurors. But the rape case had to be terminated due to mis-trial. The captive went free." The story is true.

The man who used to be "bad" and was punished is now "sick" and is changed. On the one old hand he was a bad man, on the other new hand, no man at all. The prisoners of America's progressive prisons are being driven insane. They will soon resemble the madmen who keep them and program them. Prison, like school, work, government, church, play, and profit is getting to be a *total institution*. It demands the obedience of all, it assumes the involvement of all. That is blasphemy. That is the rising of the beast. And when it approaches nigh unto the seat of the human soul, that is the beast standing in the holy of holies.

Yes, there is brutality in prison. There is beating in prison. There is rape in prison. There is slavery in prison. There is overwork in prison. There is bad food in prison. There is bad health in prison. Yes, it is true. But.

But some actual prisoners don't know they are in prison. I literally have to remind some of my clients of the fact. Yes, it is true. But.

There is prison in school.

There is prison in work.

There is prison in play.

There is prison in church.

There is prison at home.

There is good news. There is the old lady on the jury. There is the great Victory already won. There is life over dealth. *Hallelujah.*

But there is yet the Cross, there is the pathway to life. Do you see it in the old lady? Do you see it in you? Do you see yourself walking into a school-house some day for the same Jesus-name reason that the Priests walked into the draft hall in sleepy Catonsville? Luke 4:19.

Praise the Lord!

The Good News from God in Jesus Is Freedom to the Prisoners

Will D. Campbell

James Y. Holloway

So he came to Nazareth, where he had been brought up, and went to the synagogue on the Sabbath day as he regularly did. He stood up to read the lesson and was handed the scroll of the prophet Isaiah. He opened the scroll and found the passage which says,

> 'The spirit of the Lord is upon me because he has anointed me; he has sent me to announce good news to the poor, to proclaim release for prisoners and recovery of sight for the blind; to let the broken victims go free, to proclaim the year of the Lord's favor.'

He rolled up the scroll, gave it back to the attendant, and sat down; and all eyes in the synagogue were fixed on him.

He began to speak: 'Today,' he said, 'in your very hearing this text has come true.' There was a general stir of admiration; they were surprised that words of such grace should fall from his lips. 'Is not this Joseph's son?' they asked. Then Jesus said, 'No doubt you will quote the proverb to me, "Physician, heal yourself," and say, "We have heard of all your doings at Capernaum; do the same here in your own home town." I tell you this,' he went on: 'no prophet

is recognized in his own country. There were many
widows in Israel, you may be sure, in Elijah's time,
when for three years and six months the skies never
opened, and famine lay hard over the whole country;
yet it was to none of those that Elijah was sent, but
to a widow at Sarepta in the territory of Sidon.
Again, in the time of the prophet Elisha there were
many lepers in Israel, and not one of them was
healed, but only Naaman, the Syrian.' At these words
the whole congregation were infuriated. They leapt
up, threw him out of the town, and took him to the
brow of the hill on which it was built, meaning to
hurl him over the edge. But he walked straight
through them all, and went away. (Lk. 4:16-30)

*   *   *

One of the criminals who hung there with him
taunted him: 'Are not you the Messiah? Save yourself, and us.' But the other rebuked him: 'Have you
no fear of God? You are under the same sentence
as he. For us it is plain justice; we are paying the
price for our misdeeds; but this man has done nothing wrong.' And he said, 'Jesus, remember me when
you come to your throne.' He answered, 'I tell you
this: today you shall be with me in Paradise.' (Lk.
23:39-43)

Why did Jesus use that Isaiah passage to an-
nounce that the news from God was *good*?

Talk to prisoners. Be a prisoner. Here is the
clear account of what Jesus says about prisoners and
prisons. It is not we Christians on the outside—safe
with our money, respectability and connections—
who tell the prisoners the Scriptures. It is the prisoners who tell us. This is what this book is all about.

Jesus read a passage of Gospel from Isaiah, and
announced that God was coming through on His
promises, reconciling all men to each other, and to
Himself. The hatred, warfare and death between and
among us is over: God is with us the way He is with

us in Jesus. The promises, "fulfilled in your hearing"
in Jesus, come not in law, but in life. The promises
are not about moral principles, but people; not gen-
eralizations, but specifics; not pieties about God, and
man, but deeds between them. *Immanuel! God* with
us! God with us, not "for-example-prisoners," but
with prisoners, specifically, literally. A concrete deed
as a first notice about the meaning of reconciliation.
Freedom to prisoners!

The announcement then, and now, throws us into
fear, trembling and terror because it shatters our
worship of self; that is, our money, career, social
security, law-abidingness, morality, education, politics and culture. It is the announcement from God
which frightens us to install new locks on our doors,
burglar bars on our windows, sign up in the neighborhood security system, submit to more taxes for
more police protection, abrogate lofty, school-book
political principles about individual rights and due
process, and believe that everything that is against
our middle-income morality is political conspiracy
or organized crime. In Jesus God proclaims freedom
for those in prison. The prisoners are to be turned
loose. Literally. This is good news *from God.* In
Jesus God is not reform. Not rehabilitation. Not
parole. In Jesus God is freedom. Liberation. Freedom to the criminals inside the walls of stone and
so to criminals on the outside who use prison as a
shield against what is done against one another,
against God, and against the criminals who are hidden from sight inside the walls of stone.

Jesus' news is specific, immediate, indifferent to
moral codes. It is an event as close to us as brothers,
children, neighbors, bedrooms and bars and the poor
and black who stand as judgment on our citizenship

and our confessions about Jesus as Lord. *Criminals* are proclaimed free by God's deed in Jesus, and that, literally: *"Today* in your very hearing this text has come true." It is difficult to be more specific than that. We do not believe that Jesus was speaking of enlightened chaplains who, using the latest techniques of pastoral counselling, lead the prisoners into an adjustment—into a life of great books, celibacy, good behavior points. Nor was He talking of the chaplains who through the art of preaching win a soul here and there to a decision which says, "I am free wherever I am, for 'if God be for us who can be against us?' " What Jesus is talking about is unlocking the doors, dismissing the Warden and all his staff, recycling the steel bars into plowshares, and turning the prisoners loose. But let us be clear at all points. This means James Earl Ray as well as Angela Davis; William Calley as well as Phil and Dan Berrigan. So, this volume has articles by burglars, Klansmen, draft-card burners, etc., etc. . . .

Of course Jesus' neighbors in the congregation at Nazareth were dismayed and angry: *"Today* in your very hearing this text has come true." The *one* thing society cannot do is free the prisoners. Society can only *make* prisoners, and rehabilitate, adjust and then parole them . . . *to itself.* Society cannot free the prisoners. Thus does Jesus' word from God undermine the claims of absolutism lurking in all political orders—whether religious (Judah or Israel) or secular (Rome or the United States of America). All any political order can do is rest its legitimacy and make its distinctions between criminals and free men on the basis of power deals and arrangements. It is never good news to say to those who stake their

lives on the political order and its distinctions that
God frees the prisoners: Now, and here, not there
and later. God announces freedom to prisoners.
Literally, not symbolically. That is how God in Jesus
overcomes society. No guns. No plastic bombs or
napalm or anti-personnel missiles. No conspiracy
that will have to be tried in a court of law. In Jesus
God is freedom to the prisoners. Society is overcome.
Not destroyed. Overcome.

In his time Jesus had to be condemned by religion and the State. God was made a prisoner and
executed. To good religious people, as a religious
fanatic; to good citizens, as a political "king." But
in any case, he had to go. Society's law in both
religious and political dimensions makes Jesus a
prisoner and executes him in the company of other
criminals. And as a wise man reminds us, there, at
Jesus' crucifixion at the place called The Skull, there
"was the first Christian fellowship, the first certain,
indissoluble and indestructible Christian community
. . . directly and unambiguously affected by Jesus'
promise and his assurance . . . to live by this promise
is to be a Christian community." Thus, in their time
John the Baptist was a criminal, a prisoner, and executed so; thus Paul, Peter and others in the earliest
communities who confessed Jesus as Lord; thus the
prophets through whom God had spoken his words
of reconciliation "to our fathers of old." Prison and
the threat of prison were the necessary part of
the life of Jeremiah, Amos, Isaiah, Micah, Joseph,
Sampson. . . . The news that God proclaims freedom
to the prisoners is the word that overcomes society
and politics. It is the word and deed of freedom
which overcomes the words and deeds of inhumanity.

Society and politics can *only* answer by Crucifixion, as God answers Crucifixion by freedom, liberation, resurrection.

The accounts which appear in this volume say much the same thing about prisons and prisoners that one can hear in the Bible and from Jesus. Prison is all that society and law know to do when there are violations of codes, values, moralities, prejudices. Society and society's law cannot acquit, liberate, reconcile, free, resurrect. Rehabilitation? What would the prisoners be "rehabilitated" *from?* And *to? From* the very codes, values, arrangements, moralities and prejudices which put them in prison? *To* a society that sees men—all men or any man—as sovereign over these codes, values, arrangements, moralities and prejudices? Never. Society can *only* "rehabilitate" the man *from* himself and his violations of the codes which placed him in prison, and *to* the society which lives by these codes. That is all society can ever know to do to those it judges "criminals." Jesus' word about this arrangement is not that it is "bad" and must therefore be destroyed, but that it is inhuman, unfree, of the order of necessity, death . . . but, that God overcomes it.

So the proclamation about freedom to the prisoners: the news from God in Jesus is *an other* word, a Word about, and to, men. Prisoners are proclaimed free, delivered from the walls of stone: a paradigm, a first-sign, but a literal one, to all men, inside and out of prison, a notification about the specifics of the Gospel—specifics, according to Paul, that occur "while still in life . . . a new order has already begun." It is the good news from God that is an outrage: a concrete action. A deed. Freedom. Resurrection.

So the Bible looks at prisons without illusion. Their accounts of men in prison, and why they are in prison, are straightforward, without rhetoric, whether men are imprisoned by Philistines or Israelites, Babylonians, Judeans or Romans. No explanation is to be found, nor is one needed, about violations of due process or about a system of justice gone mad under the pressure of external enemies or internal tyrannies. Both Testaments understand *all* prisoners to be *political* prisoners. Murderers, rapists, sodomists, insurrectionists, assassins, thieves of millions in a stock fraud or of a loaf of bread to keep the family alive—the only thing society can do with those it judges criminals is to make prisoners. Therefore, to the Scriptures, it is always, in Dr. Menninger's phrase, "the crime of punishment,"—a situation more characterized by inhumanity's necessity than by a deliberate and evil conspiracy.

We believe that is what the essays in this volume are saying. Calmly, without hysteria. Sadly, despondently perhaps; bitterness purged by exhaustion. Without illusion about the possibility of the meaning of prison "reform." And here, perhaps, a word is in order. We have been at work on this project for more than a year. Most of the essays were written before the deaths at Attica and San Quentin, and elsewhere. (But "what was new about Attica and San Quentin?") Some of the authors have used their own names; in some cases it seemed to us best to make changes there. But, that's all we've changed. We asked these men and women to write to us about their life in prison. They did, and we've let it stand. Prison is not and never has been playing under the yum-yum tree of George Raft and James Cagney, Stalag 17 or "Johnny Cash at Folsom Prison"

(Stereo). Some of those who have written are still in prison. Some are now on parole. Some are free. Without the help of some friends and agencies, this book would not have come out the way it has, so we are deeply grateful to them, and we'll be glad to furnish leads to anyone who wants to know about prisoners from these friends and agencies. And of course there are others, well-known, and God-knows deserving of everyone's interest, who are involved in the tough and urgent task of reforming prisons.

We have worked with some of these writers more closely than with others. Yet, the baffling thing, the disconcerting thing, to those of us on the outside, is the consistent lack of bitterness against those of us who are "outside" and who now seek to drain from them the elements of their prison experiences so that we may, perhaps, for a brief time, "understand" prisoners whose freedom Jesus announced as a first-sign of the good news from God.

And this takes us back to Jesus, and to Calvary. We believe that those who are speaking to us in these pages tell us very plainly what Jesus was saying about prisoners and prisons when he spoke to the congregation at Nazareth, in his accounts of the final judgment (Matthew 25), and at Calvary. We hear no call for prison reform. We do not find instructions to the disciples to become involved in prison reform. Visit the prisoners, yes. But visit them as the prisoners Jesus talked about: no questions asked about their "crimes," about their "motives," else we tell a lie about the quality of the good news from God. Here is *another* basis for "visit the prisoners," inasmuch as those separated from the Lord at the final judgment would have visited the prisoners had they known that *Jesus the Lord* was in jail. Yet, they didn't, and we don't, because we deny the Lord is a criminal. "Visit the prisoners" has never been taken seriously by the churches. Yet, we constantly discover men and women who have been in various types of prisons for decades without *one single visitor* having signed their record card. We have suggested on other occasions that each institutional church adopt three prisoners purely and simply for purposes of visitation—so that at least once each week every man and woman and child behind bars could have one human being with whom he could have community, to whom the prisoner could tell his story. And the visitor his. We have advocated that because we are convinced that this elementary act of charity alone would provide all the prison reform that society could tolerate. And we're not talking about visiting Phil and Dan—in truth, they "visit" us when we talk to them in prison, not we, them—but about visiting the poor and the unknown and forgotten. For brutality and injustice is meted out far less often to those the world is watching than to those who are ignored by the world.

But it is not of reform that our Scriptures speak. Rather, it is that prisoners remind us again that Jesus is not a social reformer. So neither were (and are) those who call him *Lord! Lord!* God's good news in Jesus to the prisoners calls us to the reality that Jesus means *freedom,* not *reform.* That is what Jesus' life *is,* and does. Those who call him *Lord! Lord!* are ambassadors of, witnesses to, freedom to the prisoners, not messengers of reform of prisons. (The fate of the Quaker "reforms" in an earlier century might serve as a plumb-line for the realism of the Gospel at this point.)

Perhaps it is not good news to Jewish or Roman

or even our society to proclaim freedom to those whom society has made prisoners. Perhaps it is to blur if not reject the distinctions between innocent and guilty on which societies necessarily exist. Those who call him *Lord! Lord!* should never forget what happened when Jesus first spoke about freedom to the prisoners. He was speaking to his own people, his friends and neighbors and relatives: ". . . they were infuriated. They leapt up, threw him out of the town, and took him to the brow of the hill on which it was built, meaning to hurl him over the edge"— the town, *his* town, Nazareth, like all towns, built on moralities, prejudices, codes, fears, power arrangements, prestige and a worship of security. And finally Jesus' people, religious and secular people, did the only thing they knew to do with him: make him a criminal, imprison him, and execute him along with others they had judged criminals and prisoners.

And that is why the news from God in Jesus is good. All society knows to do about its criminals and prisoners is to do what they did to Jesus and to those executed with him. But God in Jesus did and does free the prisoners. Resurrection. Jesus is prisoner in *our* place. He is executed in *our* place. So that we might be free. So that we might be resurrected. "Free"? Yes, free to be with God and with neighbors and enemies the way Jesus was with God and with neighbors and enemies. But free also in and from prisons of stone and concrete.

The texts, but more critically the lives of Jesus and the prisoners admit of no demythologizing, no re-mythologizing, no hermeneutic contortions, no theologizing about symbolic or other hidden meanings. Jesus proclaims freedom to the prisoner. That is the good news in its first-fruits. Men's crimes

against God and therefore against society are taken
up, they are assumed by the imprisoned and the
executed Jesus. Jesus in *our* place. But we in *His*.
Free. Resurrected. So why not "free the prisoners"?
God has. All of us, inside and outside prison.
"Worldly standards have ceased to count in our esti-
mate of any man" (II Corinthians 5:16). So what
could the "prisoners" freed do to us that we are not
already doing to ourselves? Murder us? Pervert us?
Steal from us? Use us? Lie to us? Is not the freedom
that Jesus means the very option to humanity that
the murderer, conspirator, dope-pusher and user,
sodomist and thief cannot find in the prisons and the
paroles of society?

It seems to us that this is what Jesus is saying.
And so must we who call him *Lord! Lord!* It is not
to oppose "reform" of prison life, but to overcome
prison, to preach and live the good news of freedom
to the prisoners as a first-fruit of freedom to us all.

We cannot blot out Christmas and Easter. Jesus
became a criminal and prisoner of society and was
executed for *us. All! Everyone!* When we call him
Lord! Lord! we are therefore calling upon a Lord
who was and is a prisoner after the same manner of
those who speak to us in the pages above. It is for
them, as for the criminals who were executed with
him, that Jesus died and was raised to life. We cannot take refuge in our law-abidingness, our good
citizenship and economics, for our Lord was himself
executed as a criminal and thus brings freedom,
resurrection, to them.

If, as we believe, the first certain Christian community was those three criminals and prisoners at
their execution at Calvary, then we who call him
Lord! Lord! must bear witness to His promise to

the criminals and prisoners: "I tell you this: today you shall be with me in Paradise."

The good news from God in Jesus is freedom to the prisoners.